Lifting the Fog

Curiosity, Inspiration, and
Romance on Happy trails

Siegfried Beckedorf

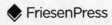

Suite 300 - 990 Fort St
Victoria, BC, v8v 3K2
Canada

www.friesenpress.com

Copyright © 2017 by Siegfried Beckedorf
First Edition — 2017

All rights reserved.

No part of this publication may be reproduced in any form, or by any means, electronic or mechanical, including photocopying, recording, or any information browsing, storage, or retrieval system, without permission in writing from FriesenPress.

Rudolph Steiner's GOETHEANUM in Dornach, Switzerland is attracting people of all walks of life looking at different and new ways in the field of of education.

ISBN
978-1-5255-0208-8 (Hardcover)
978-1-5255-0209-5 (Paperback)
978-1-5255-0210-1 (eBook)

1. BODY, MIND & SPIRIT

Distributed to the trade by The Ingram Book Company

"To be yourself in a world that is trying to make you something else is the greatest accomplishment."

- Ralph Waldo Emerson

TABLE OF CONTENTS

1   PREFACE: HEALTH AND LIFESTYLE

4   SHARING IDEAS AND IDEALS

14   THE LURE OF EUROPE

21   PARIS

25   BERLIN

33   MUNICH

36   A CHANGE IN PLANS

41   ALPINE MAJESTY—INNSBRUCK

50   MILAN—ITALIAN HOSPITALITY
         AND ROMANCE

56   BASEL, SWITZERLAND,
         ON THE RIVER RHINE, BORDERED BY
         FRANCE AND GERMANY

60   STEINER'S ANTHROPOSOPHY AND
         WALDORF EDUCATION

65   INTRODUCTION TO
         THE GOETHEANUM—
         A GROWING ROMANCE UNFOLDING

81   IN AWE . . . AND CHERISH THE SOUNDS OF
         SINGING ON THE TRAIL

87	SPICING DAY-TO-DAY LIFE WITH PHILOSOPHY
91	A TRIP BACK TO CALGARY
98	NEW OPPORTUNITIES
101	LOUIS OFF TO ZURICH
102	MY PARENTS WANT TO MEET YOU
112	GOOD SIGNS IN THE WIND
117	A NEW CHAPTER TO EXPLORE AND EXPAND
121	SETTLING INTO LIFE IN SWITZERLAND
122	A VISIT ACROSS THE POND
128	BACK IN THE SADDLE IN DORNACH
129	LET THE BELLS RING
130	SWITZERLAND—HERE WE COME
133	CHANGES IN THE WIND
136	A VISIT FROM ZURICH
138	LIFTING THE FOG WITH AWARENESS
140	IN AWE—CHERISHIING THE SOUNDS ON THE TRAILS AGAIN
141	AGAIN, WEDDING BELLS RING IN DORNACH
143	THIS TIME A LURE OF REMOTE AND ANCIENT CIVILIZATIONS
145	NAMIBIA, AFRICA—HERE WE COME
147	GOBABIS
149	BACK INTO ANCIENT HISTORY, MAN'S EARLIEST ON RECORD
160	MARIENTAL

170	HARDAP DAM
173	DRIVING NORTH TO OTJIWARONGO
175	TSUMEB
177	HOBA METEORITE
178	TALERS, TALERS, TALERS
180	ETOSHA—WILDLIFE PARK
186	ON THE WAY TO CROSSING THE OLDEST DESERT IN THE WORLD
188	SWAKOPMUND ON THE ATLANTIC
198	AN ADVENTUROUS SHORTCUT TO WINDHOEK
200	WINDHOEK, THE CAPITAL OF NAMIBIA
204	AT 30,000 FEET ABOVE AFRICA
206	BACK IN SWITZERLAND
209	A GREAT MOMENT— A NEW ROLE IN SHARING STEINER'S PHILOSOPHY
210	INTERNATIONAL EXPERIENCES
212	A CHANGE OF PACE
213	CELEBRATING URSULA'S LIFE
214	THE CALL OF THE FOOTHILLS
215	AN EXPANDING NETWORK WITH EMPHASIS ON SCIENCE
217	Acknowledgements

PREFACE: HEALTH AND LIFESTYLE

Eric, now in his eighties, is active and creative, and maintains a sense of curiosity and humor. He kept up communication with colleagues, students, and friends, expanding their newsletters in Europe and North America. At a meeting in the US, a colleague once said, "You travelled a lot and widened your horizon in education and philosophy. At your age, you are very active in many fields including the newsletter with its widespread readership. How do you do that?" Eric replied confidently. "I believe, and I have maintained the belief throughout the years, that I am responsible for my physical and mental health, unless circumstances beyond my control change that. A positive attitude in day-to-day life also supports my responsibility."

The colleague asked him how he meets unexpected challenges around health and other things. Eric replied with a deep breath that a constant awareness of the invisible universal energy present within him and us all builds inner strength. "I let it happen. We are more than what society generally tells us. Breathing consciously, I let this energy flow from head to toe. We are all part of this energy, its power and mystery. It feels great."

Apparently impressed, his colleague replied that in his position as a high school teacher, he believed it would be worthwhile to bring the concepts of taking responsibility, engaging in exercise, and adopting a practice of conscious breathing into the classroom at an early age. Eric agreed.

A generally positive person, Eric Schiller felt that this point in his advancing age was the time to wake up and develop new habits. Knowing his bones suffered from wear and tear, he tried to feel his pain. He had been advised to accept pain, to "lean into it, notice pain fading." Still, that took some time to practise. His doctor told him an accident in his thirties was the cause of his knee problems. His bones had not been set right after the operation and adjustments were neglected. A knee replacement may be the answer. Eric caught himself here doing what he calls "accepting what is." He got treatment after a long waiting period and an assessment prior to the operation, which was successful. Intensive physiotherapy brought him back to his feet and he carried on with his favourite mental and physical activities.

Eric reflected often on how his life had changed after his wife had died, only a year before. Being present while she made her transition, Eric felt a tremendous sense of loss and sadness, but also good

Lifting the Fog

fortune at having shared an exciting life with Ursula for many years.

Eric was not letting anything negative affect his lifestyle, and he maintained a good sense of humour. Why not choose to be positive? He knew that such an attitude would be healthier than looking at life through dark glasses. He practised living in the present moment, one in which his state of consciousness was the observer of body and mind, using the body and mind as amazing tools to be used and observed. The past is gone and the future not yet here. Although focusing on the body through diet and exercise can be helpful, the real shift has to be in consciousness.

SHARING IDEAS
AND IDEALS

At about this time, Eric's attention was drawn to a book called *The Good Book*, by A. C. Grayling, which raised his curiosity in his search for meaning in life. In pursuing physical exercise, Eric met a fellow student at a gym. Louis LaSalle, of French Canadian background, was irritated about being too much in a hurry to follow the exercise program. With a good sense of humour, Eric replied, "Maybe going for walks and getting some fresh air is the answer instead."

Louis, told him impatiently, "I was told to do exercise to lose weight."

"Are you not the boss?" Eric smiled at him when Louis mumbled that he would think about that. Even though they expressed different opinions on many subjects, the two hit it off with regular discussions of their fields of interest.

In their twenties, these two young students often discussed an uncertainty in their chosen careers. Eric had chosen to study architectural design and principles. His hobby of sketching unique structures

Lifting the Fog

led him into this field. Louis was studying natural and biological sciences with a real interest in the beauty of the natural world around him. He was impatient and often looked somewhat worried because of his uncertainty around his future. Eric was more relaxed, and would try to keep Louis calm. "Life is too short to change some peoples' attitudes," he would say. "Here is some advice I picked up somewhere: 'You think you have problems! I've got so many worries that if something happened today, I wouldn't have time to worry about it for three weeks.'" Louis's face brightened. "That is a good one. Can I have it?"

On another occasion, Louis remarked that he had become aware of an enormous amount of new knowledge entering science and technology at a rapid pace, and said he was getting frustrated by it. He felt he couldn't keep up with it. But Eric maintained a fairly steady conviction about trying to live in the moment, doing the best he knew. Normally, their dialogue was full of humour and respectful of each other's views. Louis, at one point in an exchange of ideas, told Eric, "You know I read a lot in the best-selling thrillers to give my studies a change of pace. But lately, I catch myself looking at life in the present moment, as you mentioned you are trying to do. I feel it is almost like a thrill or a spark to become aware of what lies deep within me. I am trying to pay attention to 'gamification,' which seems, in some circles, to be creating a real inter-est in putting your personal goals on the internet, gaming, and promoting creativity. It is a growing awareness of our inner strength, an uplifting feeling of individuality." To that, Eric added: "Recently, my attention was drawn to *The Good Book*, by A. C. Grayling, professor of philosophy at U of London, which devotes many pages to the natural power within us, a sensible approach to human potential. I will bring it along to our next get-together, as well as a fascinating book by Gary Zukav, *The Dancing Wu Li Masters: A Look at the New Physics*, so we can share our understanding. I am sure you will like it." Louis was excited. "Please do."

The opportunity to meet was seen through when the two decided to go camping over a weekend to discuss items of mutual interest. Louis brought along a book by Bruce Lipton, Ph.D., *The Biology of Belief*. Comparing titles and contents, Louis mentioned, "We need to spend a month in the mountains to digest these books. Let us deal with the highlights only."

Louis started out. "According to this book, there are current studies telling us that our lifestyles and attitudes influence the flow of activity of our cells, the amazing network of the micro-functions in our body. Scientists maintain that about fifty trillion cells interact constructively within each of our bodies. Genetics are not as rigid as we learned only two decades ago. We influence our cells with our thoughts, lifestyle, and environment. This book opened my eyes to fascinating new thinking." When Eric picked up his two books, he said, "This

Lifting the Fog

book here, by A. C. Grayling, I read it to you. What really caught my attention was this paragraph: 'For a secular age in which many find that religion no longer speaks to them, *The Good Book* is a literary tour de force—a book of life and practice invoking the greatest minds of the past in the perennial challenge of being human.' And this one here by Gary Zukav, *The Dancing Wu Li Masters*, offers a new look at 'the new physics." I often re-read this, but I will leave that for a later discussion." Louis and Eric carried on reflecting on their own lives and how new or different thinking was affecting their current existence.

They kept their dialogue active during the following two years and maintained their stand with a sense of good humour and the exchange of daily experiences. At a political meeting they both attended, one man stood up, very excited, and shouted, "This is political crap! It is time we blow our horn!" Now Louis got up. "Yeah, I agree. We do not have to put up with that. Let's all blow our whistle and stop this nonsense." Eric looked at Louis in surprise and told him, "Now, I know you could become a politician! Maybe that is your direction, not science. In politics, you can have fun shouting, 'let's all blow our whistle!'"

"Well," Louis replied, "what do you call this political crap?"

"Fooling the public, although I do not fully understand their logic," Eric smiled. But Louis was very

Siegfried Beckedorf

emotional "It is crap!" he said, before conceding that keeping a calm head is better for one's health.

At another of their meetings, Eric asked, "How can you determine that life is meaningful?" Louis answered with a smile, "You climb a ladder step by step, each step giving you a new idea or a new silly one to look at closely and see if it is meaningful. See? That is my wisdom." Eric was impressed. "But how do you know it is meaningful?" Louis now perked up. "When I feel it in my bones, my veins, my cells. It is an intuitional prodding, like you mentioned recently, bringing hidden diamonds to light."

Now Eric showed he was really impressed. Louis carried on emphasizing the importance of stopping in his tracks once in a while, that smelling the flowers puts him in harmony with nature's rhythm and energy, and lets him see life as it is. Eric was in awe. "These words come from your heart, Louis." Louis appreciated Eric's comments.

In the meantime, girlfriends joined their conversations. The growing movement of women sharing in the power of business and in all walks of life added to lively exchanges of ideas. The young ladies expressed a lot of disappointment about the lack of input during classes around human potential. Louis advised them to get together with other students and speak to the teachers with suggestions. "We tried," one of the girls, said. "But my teacher is arrogant. He shrugged his shoulders."

"Ignoring your suggestion is serious disregard. Blow your horn or, better, your whistle!" Louis got

Lifting the Fog

excited, but remained calm. "How does that help?" Louis was in his element in his efforts to explain that this is their future, and that they want the best education they can get. That ended their discussion.

A year later, Eric and Louis went on another weekend camping trip to get a chance to talk. Eric mentioned that he was getting concerned about the amount of new research entering the field of technology, and how that was affecting his focus on his own path of endeavour. "Stay away from multitasking" was Louis's comment." But Eric was lost in his thoughts, so Louis carried o.n "Let your heart decide what you take out of the basket of new knowledge. Why do we have to stick to old ways of getting stuffed with knowledge? The word *education* has Latin roots: educare /educe, which means drawing latent, inherent knowledge (out of students), not stuffing it in."

Eric hummed, "you need to be stuffed to learn."

"Oh," Louis disagreed. "You and I, all of us, have an inherent gift, a talent that's part of our individuality, which makes us creative. A teacher has to respect that and encourage our creativity. We want to participate with his delivery of textbook knowledge to us, but we don't want it stuffed into us. Our individuality for interpretation has to be respected. We have to blow our whistle." Eric was impressed. "You are a wise man, Louis," he said. "But how in heaven do you expect the educational system to be responsive to your ideas?"

Siegfried Beckedorf

"I read between the lines. Changes are in the wind." Louis was serious and Eric made fun of him. That ended their conversation. Eric could not stop thinking about Louis's determination and decided to look into the meaning of education. His curiosity about the subject of individuality and originality was soon preoccupying Eric. *Isn't this leading to an egoistic attitude?* he asked himself. But on further study, he concluded that if he wasn't sure of himself, he couldn't convince anybody else. And he didn't consider himself an egoistic when he could potentially help others to see it his way and let them get their own act together before making any judgments.

A quote by Ralph Waldo Emerson made Eric think: "To be yourself in a world that is trying to make you something else is the greatest accomplishment." Who am I? he wondered. A conscious human being like anybody else. I may be different than everyone because of my genes, my environment and upbringing, my education, and my experiences. But we all are part of this great energy, this immense power of nature. To be true to ourselves is a learning experience, a challenge we all have. Oh, but that analysis made Eric feel good. Next, he considered whether we need to "blow our whistle" to bring about changes in the present educational way of "stuffing," as Louis had declared it, to allow respect for our individuality? Changes in the past have been achieved with time and patience, he noted, but also with constant prodding.

— 10 —

Lifting the Fog

Eric settled down, his head full of encouraging ideas. Sharing them with Louis would only reinforce his impatience with what the future holds for him. On one occasion, Louis told Eric, "Listen, you are taking your search for solutions in slow motion. There are changes in the wind and we can be the flag bearers!" Louis stood his ground. But a few days later, Eric and Louis had another chat. This time, Eric explained his concern about the change a high school student experiences when he goes away to university or to a technical institution, and starts thinking about his future. We know the general thinking of parents and others about going to university is that it's the thing to do, the thing that lets you make more money. But in my opinion, that decision should be made by the high school student before leaving school, firstly to see through his own dream to follow his heart. Achieving true happiness with that decision may take a few years for the student. But, then, what rush is there? It is his own future." Louis followed Eric's reasoning. "I know this is what bothers me often about my own future. I may change my course—I don't know yet."

Eric, some fellow students, and two teachers were invited to a conference in the US for exchanging ideas and new technology. Eric liked the idea. New materials would be introduced with environmental benefits. One of the American teachers led the topic of their meeting to new materials with samples and demonstrated new processes of manufacturing. He emphasized that it is the responsibility of

— 11 —

students and teachers alike to check the economics of hugely higher prizes and benefits to the consumers. A lively discussion followed. In the afternoon, someone else picked up the subject of corruption and lack of ethics. Eric was surprised and pleased. Then the Canadian teacher tuned in and confirmed signs of changes aimed at stemming corruption and encouraging ethics in research and business. Eric asked an American student sitting next to him to whom he introduced himself, named Frank, with this question: "How widespread is this concern in American colleges?"

"It is a growing concern, as far as I know. It involves politics and government, so it's therefore difficult to assess. We students need to speak up. With growing environmental concerns worldwide, I have lately thought that contamination of building materials is not the only problem. We need to add corruption and lack of ethics to contamination of our minds."

Eric agreed. "That is an interesting point; it makes sense."

"Yes, the time has come. It is a worldwide problem. The internet may be the way for our generation to get international attention." Frank seemed to be very serious. "Let's stay in contact," he said. Eric was encouraged and gave Frank his e-mail address. He mentioned his discussion to one of his teachers with whom he'd raised his concern earlier, saying that changes were in the wind. His reply was, "We need concrete evidence to get any attention.

Lifting the Fog

To the point of contamination of our minds, I am not holding my breath—it is a matter of individual conscience. But who can provide leadership with influence and authority? Let's find out how much support there is."

Louis was excited when Eric discussed his trip to the US with him." Maybe I'll write an article in our student journal." Louis replied with impatience, "as I told you, the signs of change are in the air."

"Yes, Louis. I am holding my breath, checking the air." Jokingly, Louis demonstrated breathing in deeply.

THE LURE OF EUROPE

A few busy months passed before the friends met again. Any mention of their concerns about corruption and ethics had subsided. The subject was still on their minds, but it had been overtaken by more immediate other concerns. Louis's impatience was still evident when he brought up the idea of taking some time off from his studies. "I need to reinforce my interest in my studies, to not get into a rut." He was pondering the idea of traveling to Europe when he met with Eric who, in turn, surprised himself by taking an interest in this subject. Eric had similar ideas to put more fun and enjoyment into his studies. "Oh, what's your time plan?" Louis was also surprised that Eric showed interest." Any time I can round up the money. I may do some part-time work, like driving a truck." "I want to finish this year," Eric replied, "to get an important part of my studies behind me. Besides, a trip would require a lot of planning and money. How about going for three weeks—Europe is expensive? Also, which countries to visit and how to travel?"

Lifting the Fog

"I have no idea and no preference." Louis, without much thought, listed France, Germany, Austria, Italy, and Greece, but said that three weeks seemed too short for him.

The following months went by quickly. In the meantime, Eric stayed in touch with Frank, the American student he had met on business. This fellow had kept his word and e-mailed Eric once in a while. One of the messages included Eric's plan to travel to Europe. Frank replied, "If you have a chance to travel to Basel, Switzerland, look at the amazing design of architecture and materials at the Goetheanum, designed by the Austrian-born Rudolf Steiner and named after Johann Wolfgang von Goethe. This unique building houses the Society's research and educational facilities. He also designed a second one. I know from my talk with you that this would interest you." A reference to Steiner's well-known role as the founder of the Waldorf Schools was enclosed, as well. Eric received detailed descriptions and put it into a folder to take along to Europe. Why not? he told himself. I have to discuss that with Louis.

Louis mentioned to Eric that the trip to Europe may also give them opportunities to learn how ethics and corruption may be evident as a concern among students over there. Eric was getting more and more excited about the trip. "You know, Louis," he said. "This trip is a bigger thing than I originally thought. It may change our expectations of the future, open our eyes, widen our horizons., maybe even see us holding our breath, considering the unexpected."

"That's OK with me," Louis agreed. Eric added, "I mean, we may find benefits from our experiences in Europe to apply in our careers in Canada."

At one of their planning meetings, Eric became thoughtful. They could, he said, travel to India, Egypt, or any other country. Europe represented an inspiration to go back to their roots. For instance, Louis's ancestors came from France and were early pioneers in fur trading in the 1600s in Quebec and Ontario. His parents trace their heritage back from early German settlers in Texas on his father's side, and his mother is proud of a long British heritage. Yet they immigrated to English-speaking Canada. Eric's interest was in history. In a nutshell, northern Europe to him was mainly Great Britain, France, and Germany. Southern Europe adds variety to a population of about 375 million people. Great Britain represents three parts: Metropolitan London, the centre of the country; the seat of royalty; and the rural population with its industry and agriculture. Then there is Scotland. The Scots opened the doors for the British Empire to unfold with their exploratory nature. That is probably also why they long for independence. A visit to Great Britain is also a good idea.

Eric spelled out his ideas to Louis. "France used to be a colonial power. The French Revolution gave Europe a sense of freedom from royalty and more power to the citizens. It changed France in many

Lifting the Fog

ways. Their lifestyle is so different and more relaxed in comparison to that of the British and the German.

"Germany used to be a country that was split into, I think, about forty-eight states until Bismarck, the Iron Chancellor, came on the scene to unite Germany and bring industrial revolution and social welfare to their people. The black spot of the Nazi period is fixed in Germany's history—twelve years of a terrible period. Today it is a strong democracy and a leading economic power within the European Union. These are just the historic differences." Louis repeated, "We will have a chance to experience the differences. I like that."

Preparations went smoothly. Ideas ran through Eric's mind. "A few days in Paris for sightseeing, then to Berlin to get in on the international attention that city had experienced lately, then to Salzburg, Austria, close to the German border. Through Italy by bus and via ship to Greece. In between, we may want to be flexible to make changes." What a handful! Eric was really excited when the day arrived for departure, whereas Louis was slow in getting his mind and luggage organized.

The eight-hour flight over the continent was seemingly endless. The Canadian prairies, the Canadian Shield, and across the Atlantic was exciting, but also tiring. Suddenly the attention of passengers turned to a young couple shouting at each other in a heated argument, the mother shaking her crying baby violently. Eric and Louis were close by and very disturbed. They called for a stewardess.

Siegfried Beckedorf

When she came, she asked the couple to vacate their seats and got help moving them to the back of the plane, while the arguments continued.

At this moment, the situation turned ugly. The husband wiggled himself out of the grip of the male attendant and produced what looked like a pistol! The mother was terrified! The pilot was forced to act quickly. The nearest airport, in Reykjavik, was notified of an emergency landing. The husband screamed at his wife and at the attendant who, with great strength, removed the pistol. The passengers were kept in control while the man was subdued and put in handcuffs. Eric and Louis were very much on alert and tried to calm the passengers, as well. Eric turned to Louis and said, "I am holding my breath. It was a close call, a tragedy prevented." "Yeah," was all Louis could add. The landing was well organized. Husband, wife, and baby were picked up by police. The passengers were informed of a short stay and the flight attendant brought the passengers up to date. She also provided a brief description of the City of Reykjavik and the island's massive hot water springs that provide energy to the city's residents. The beauty of the lava-covered mountains was quite evident. The plane took off after all the systems were checked.

Back at 30,000 feet, the passengers were relaxed, looking down on the island. It was like waking up from a dream. Eric unpacked a book to read. Louis was curious and looked at the title: *The Art of Stillness*, by Pico Iyer (original copyright 1951 to

Lifting the Fog

1983), a new issue. He also had a little booklet to remind readers to "Breathe consciously."

"Oh, interesting. You mean something like 'Stop in your tracks and smell the flowers,'" Louis said, taking a real interest. "Exactly. You know, the author talks about training executives in large American corporations in meditation, on how to become still once in a while, to clear their minds and become, in time, more creative, productive, and generally happier employees." Louis showed what he brought along: *Scientists Confront Creationism*. From leading natural scientists and educators, this is a decisive rebuttal to those who undermine science in the name of religion with overwhelming scientific evidence for evolution. Eric looked at it with great interest and said, "We will not be bored!" Louis had the same idea. "On the same line, I have another book in case we have lots of time, *The Hidden Connections*, by Fritjof Capra on "the science for sustainable living." Now they turned their attention to the view as the pilot announced, "Thank you all for keeping calm in the situation we just experienced. We are back at 30,000 feet, now approaching Scotland." Eric turned to Louis. "Breathe consciously," he said, "at 30,000 feet in space!" Louis did, and both got lost in their thoughts. Looking into seemingly empty space, Louis wondered about definitions of eternity and infinity—the fathomless depth.

"This is almost scary to think about, but I have a seatbelt on to stay put."

Siegfried Beckedorf

"Oh, yeah?" Eric replied with a smile. Louis was serious.

In a relatively short time, they flew over some of the Shetland Islands of Scotland, and across the North Sea and the Netherlands, to land in Amsterdam. Amsterdam, from the air, lay sprawled out beneath them. The neat rows of fields, greenhouses, canals, and housing were surprising.

Eric and Louis heard later about the incident over Iceland. The press praised the efforts of the flight crew and passengers to avoid any panic. The man in question was put on trial, the mother and baby put into a temporary shelter.

PARIS

Fully excited by the crowd, if a bit overwhelmed by it, they took the train through heavily populated areas via Brussels as well as the mixed agricultural country of Belgium and northern France to Paris. Louis was deep in thought when he mentioned that this part of Europe had been heavily damaged during both World Wars. "It looks quite peaceful now." It was tempting for the two to spend money in the city's inviting open-air restaurants. They agreed to keep an eye on their budget. Louis commented, "I'll look over your shoulder and you over mine." Eric suggested that Louis control his temptation or Eric would have to bail him out. "Oh, let's see who runs out of money first!" Louis said, undisturbed.

The Arc de Triumphe in the centre of the Place of Charles de Gaulle was not to be missed. This historic monument of the Napoleonic wars was indeed attracting huge numbers of people, including, noticeably, Asian tourists with cameras. There were pigeons everywhere. A nearby pub looked inviting for the two to take a rest. Half of the seating area was exposed to the sidewalk along the boulevard.

Siegfried Beckedorf

They sat down next to what turned out to be Polish soldiers in European army outfits. A conversation in English was slow but understandable. When Eric mentioned Canada, their faces lit up. One of them mentioned relatives in Montreal. Louis asked, "How do you like Paris?"

"Wine is cheap and people are nice in the city but not so in the country."

"Why?" Louis asked.

"They do not like uniforms." When Eric asked if they were students at home on service time, they confirmed that they were. They said they wanted to get back to Poland as soon as they could. Eric mentioned they were on a trip through Europe via Berlin, Austria, and Italy. One of the Polish guys said Berlin was good to visit. It's close to Poland, good for work, and filled with young people from many countries having fun. French beer, they said, is not as good as Polish beer.

Eric turned to Louis. "Let's look for a place to stay for the night." Their map showed an area near the railway station where they had arrived. While they were looking at it outside the pub, a young couple heard them speaking English and offered some help. In English, the young French man with the heavy French accent pointed them to a place to stay for the night nearby. Louis invited them to sit for a coffee. In good English, the lady mentioned her traveling experiences through Canada as a student at the University of Quebec. Curious about this, Louis applied his limited knowledge of French to

— 22 —

Lifting the Fog

questioning her, then quickly changed to English. "Before we left Canada, my friend Eric and I were very much aware about some unrest among students in Calgary with reference to changes in the wind for students to participate in the way education is presented by teachers and professionals." This caught the young man's attention. He responded that he and his wife were studying in Paris and were aware of similar unrest among students there. Eric told him that the same concerns were afoot in the US. "Where do we go with that?" Louis piped up. "We have some support from teachers, but nobody seems to take this to the point to blow the whistle." The French student replied, "Our professors are not on the same wavelength with us and want us to stick to our curriculum. But I have the feeling that, in a year or two, this will change because of the international character now so evident in universities around the world."

The couple walked with them for a while toward the address of the youth hostel. On the way, Eric wondered about a crowd of young people lining up in front of a building with a sign reading, "Moulin Rouge, Paris." The woman told them that this is a dancing academy, one of many in most big cities around the world. She said that training new students from many countries in a particular art of dance is very popular in Paris. Once they are accepted, they can work in any Moulin Rouge in other cities. Young people like this, she told them, because it gives them opportunities to work in a

Siegfried Beckedorf

place of their choice. With that, they parted and exchanged contact information.

The youth hostel looked very clean and had rooms available. Here, Eric and Louis met a few German students from a university in Berlin who gave them some good advice about what to do in the city. For instance, they told them that accommodation and food is reasonable in the Kreuzberg and Alexander Platz areas in former East Berlin. There, they would find the Island of Museums and the beautiful Tiergarten Park. They would meet young people from all parts of South America and Africa, and especially students from China and Spanish-speaking countries. The Germans spoke fluent English and were on the way to Spain on bicycles. Eric wished them happy trails and Louis waved his hands, shouting, "See you on bicycles in Canada." The reply was: "Too big for bicycles, I think." "No," said Louis. "You will be surprised!"

BERLIN

The train trip to Berlin was fast, with no delays at the border with Germany. European Union members can travel across the Union without a pass. Even though the train moved fast, they were surprised to see so many large cities so close together. They learned that this area, the Ruhr area, was formerly a centre of heavy industry that had now been replaced by an environmental engineering centre with new office buildings and warehouses, as well as mainly agricultural and forested areas. Berlin's main station was crowded, with taxis everywhere. A taxi took them to Alexander Platz. The driver, who was of Turkish background, was fluent in English and very helpful. He took them to a four-storey older apartment with view of downtown and waited until they confirmed their stay. The sunny day made the arrival friendly.

The former East German part of Berlin had been restored after suffering bad damage during World War II. There were signs of Communist architecture in the blocks without balconies that had been renovated with large windows. The Alexander TV

Tower, the largest building in East Berlin, looked like it had been renovated. It was impressive, with many restaurants and pubs. Over lunch with bockwurst, sausage, sauerkraut, and beer on the first floor, they watched the traffic. So far, so good, Eric thought. He was pleased. "I can see the Brandenburg Gate, United Germany's Arc de Triomphe," Louis said. "It's located in the former West Berlin. According to the literature, the Potsdamer Platz is the 1920s-era entertainment centre of Berlin, now with new high-rise towers downtown. It's a good spot to stay a day or two." Eric agreed.

A couple of young ladies settled down at the next table, constantly talking. Eric was curious and courageously tried a little German. "Are you Deutsch?" One woman said, "I am. My friend is Canadian and studying German history." Now Louis cut in. "Where in Canada?" "Montreal," she replied, before a waiter interrupted their conversation. After resuming their lunch, Eric pointed at a police car, rushing with its lights on to a gathering of some men in the vicinity around a parked car. It looked like a drug raid when two policemen approached and checked papers and the car's interior. Four men of Asian or African descent were interrogated. The police made a phone call and, within a few minutes, a police van appeared to take all four off. Their car was towed away. Passersby did not seem to be much interested. This took also the attention of the ladies. "That's the way it goes," the German girl pointed out in English, looking at Eric. "Are you new here, are

Lifting the Fog

you Americans?" Eric replied they were Canadians from Calgary, just arrived from Paris. "I want to visit Canada next year when my friend goes back to Montreal." Now it was Louis's turn. "It is a long way to see the rest of Canada!" She mentioned that she and her friend wanted to take a bus tour. Eric was curious and inquired about universities in Berlin. Which one was she attending? The Canadian girl replied that she was at the Free University of Berlin. "It is an open place with a lot of tolerance and very international. The Humboldt University, the one that was founded in 1810, is the oldest and is expanding a lot with a branch in Sao Paulo, Brazil. It is close to allowing some tolerance like the Free University."

"What do you mean by tolerance?" Eric asked.

"The freedom we have in selecting subjects and attending lectures." The Canadian student pointed out that the Free University was trying to follow that line, but that the professors of other specialized universities were slow and authoritative. "Ist doch Quatsch," the Germany girl interrupted. "We need our freedom of speech." Now Eric laughed. "I know the meaning of 'Quatsch.' In English, it's 'BS' or 'bullshit.'"

"Really, 'Quatsch' is fun to say. If you want to get to know a bit about the Free University, we could possibly have coffee in the lobby tomorrow morning when we have a break." They exchanged e-mails and first names and parted. Eric was pleased with how things were playing into their expectations for the trip. Louis was excited as well.

Eric and Louis took a very crowded streetcar filled with mostly young people to the Freie Universitaet. It was a huge complex of modern and older structures whose gleaming main entrance was right at the streetcar stop, making it easy for them to locate the large lobby. It took a while to spot the ladies who had reserved a place. The Canadian girl produced a file of loose-leaf sheets of information. "Here is something you may be interested in called 'gamification,'" she said. "It turns gaming on computers into fun. You can produce your own games, win points, and overcome boredom, time-wasting, and unhealthy habits. Friends and fellow students all over the world have picked up on this and developed their own software to create fun games and motivation to improve their lifestyles, studies, and careers. Oklahoma City, population 475,000, made headlines with its efforts to motivate the entire population to change their eating habits, lose weight, and improve sanitary conditions within a period of five years. And this was with their own fun-creating software! Read for yourself." She was excited and exhausted. The German girl added that this activity was going on not only among young people and students, but teachers, as well. "It may become as popular as yoga or golf." Eric and Louis were acquainted with the information lying in front of them. She mentioned that discussion groups had been formed to learn more about gamification. When the young men took their leave, the women asked them to check it out for themselves on their travels. "*Auf wiedersehen*. We

Lifting the Fog

may see you in Canada." "Thank you, thank you, for your efforts. We'll meet again," Eric said gratefully. "Happy trails, you inspiring ladies!" Louis added.

Next, Eric and Louis walked by the Museum Island, an impressive assembly of five well-known museums on the River Spree in downtown Berlin. Eric took a special interest in the evolution of the museum design and its historic significance. They did not regret an extended visit to this UNESCO National Heritage Site, but were tired and glad to arrive at their apartment only a few blocks away. Looking at their timetable for the trip, they decided to visit the Tiergarten Park the next morning, to walk along the "Unter den Linden" boulevard to the Brandenburg Gate, and to pass the former "Iron Wall" dividing the former East and West Germany to the Bundestag Building. The plan after that was to take a bus to Munich for a day or two and then the train to Salzburg, Austria.

Walking along the "Unter den Linden" boulevard, they admired the beautiful linden trees. One thousand trees were planted more than three-and-half centuries ago by Frederick the Great. They had to be replanted after being cut down after WW II when the boulevard was destroyed. It stretches a kilometre and a half and is very wide, as per its original intention as a thoroughfare for carriage rides and parades. Historic and cultural buildings lined the boulevard, including the statue of Frederick the Great, the Russian Embassy, the Humboldt University, and others. They passed through the Brandenburg Gate

— 29 —

at Pariser Platz, a photogenic symbol of victory and freedom, and also the location where the former wall dividing the two Germanys had been erected in 1961. Passing Checkpoint Charlie and looking at the literature available, Louis exclaimed, "Lots of history here!"

They visited the Reichstag, the new German parliament building. The huge glass dome was erected on the roof as a gesture to the original 1894 cupola and transparency. While walking up the impressive stairs that let visitors look at parliament in session below, Eric commented, "Can you imagine Hitler's Nazi dictatorship having ruled this country at one time?" Louis shook his head and turned his attention to the impressive 360-degree view over the city.

Louis looked at the map of downtown Berlin, concerned about the time to get to the Tiergarten. He suggested taking the rapid train. This, the "green lung of Berlin," is a huge park—520 acres. Eric got up, ready to go.

The S-Bahn, a rapid train, took them right to the centre of the Tiergarten, in front the Victory Column, a monument to commemorate the Prussian victory in the Danish-Prussian War. Louis pointed to a note in the brochure about the Berlin slang word for the monument being "the Golden Lizzie."

Eric and Louis enjoyed joining a big crowd of people of all ages, some in uniforms, some families, with baby buggies in tow behind bicycles. An information column displayed the history of the park dating back to 1527 when it was a hunting area for

Lifting the Fog

the royalty of the State of Brandenburg as well as the site of many historic buildings and statues.

Louis and Eric moved to a large gathering of people around an open stage with a British band and singers providing lively music to applause. They found a spot to sit down and enjoyed the atmosphere. Clouds moved in, and it began to rain lightly. A roof system provided the stage area with a slow-moving, half-moon-shaped canvas cover. People moved into sheltered picnic structures around the entertainment area. The music kept going. Families gathered around barbecues for picnics. Eric and Louis joined a family with two small children around a large table. The couple ask them to join them, speaking first in German then in English. Eric explained their visit and praised the beautiful surroundings. This was quite relaxing for Eric and Louis. They got more information about what could be done in the Tiergarten Park. "You can spend a couple of days here and not see all there is." It was getting late in the afternoon when Eric and Louis decided to take a detour with the rapid train via the Central Square of Potsdamer Platz.

Only one kilometre from the Brandenburger Tor (Gate), the Potsdamer Platz is an important public square in the centre of Berlin, along the former wall dividing East and West. It was rebuilt— in the largest construction project in Europe at the time— after being completely destroyed during World War II. Skyscrapers, like those of the Sony Centre and Daimler Benz, dominate. Arcades, shopping

Siegfried Beckedorf

plazas, cinemas, restaurants, and the Museum of Technology are within walking distance. A pub near an entertainment centre advertising night life was a good place for the students to have fun.

Curious about this place, Eric and Louis settled in for a rest. The lively music encouraged many couples to dance. Eric looked around. "This is tempting," he said. But it did not get Louis excited. "I am tired and want to reserve my energy for the two-kilometre walk to the apartment via the Unter den Linden Boulevard."

MUNICH

There were two options for travelling to Austria: by inner-city train to Vienna, or by bus to Munich and staying overnight. Eric looked at a map and pointed out that Munich was very close to the border with Austria. "Look, the bus will follow the Autobahn all the way to Munich—they say about nine hours for the trip, with stops in Leipzig and Nuremberg. It's a trip straight south, almost touching the border of the Czech Republic."

Leipzig is the capital of the State of Saxony, formerly East Germany, and is now Germany's boomtown, growing by 12,000 people a year and now with a population of over 500,000. The city has been a centre of cultural activities in Eastern Europe for many centuries. Leipzig was heavily damaged during WW II and has been rebuilt with a brand-new airport serving mainly Eastern Europe. It has regained its importance as a centre for book exhibitions in Germany.

The flat country changed to rolling hills, beautiful forests, and park-like settings as they approached Nuremberg. "This is where the Nazi trials took place! What a terrible time and change for the German people, but a meaningful place for the trial," Louis said, as he looked at information about the city. "This is quite a historic place, first mentioned in 1050 and expanded dramatically due to its important location on key trade routes. It's even said that Nuremberg has often been referred as to the unofficial capital of the Holy Roman Empire. It shows here a continuous reference to Nuremberg as the centre of all German states and a seat of leading royalties for many centuries. What history!"

Eric was somewhat lost in thought. "My family has a German background with a settlers' and pioneering history in Texas. At times, my father refers to the terrible Nazi period as a black spot in Germany's history. He maintains that most Germans accept responsibility and feel guilty for misunderstanding Hitler's real motives. He also emphasizes Germany's culture and economic strength in the past and after World War II as an example of solid democracy, as a part of the creation and maintenance of the European Union."

"This is what confirms what I mean with the history of Nuremberg and today's growing interest among tourists in that history," Louis said. They looked forward to having a lunch break at a restaurant featuring Nuernberger Bratwurst (grilled sausage) close to the oldest part of this city, as announced by the driver. The bus driver negotiated the narrow, winding cobblestone streets in an amazing way, with hardly any room for cars

Lifting the Fog

or trucks to pass. The restaurant offered a lot of parking spaces surrounded by small and old timber-framed houses with only narrow walkways in between. Long tables sat in a parking area under bright sunshine. Quick-service personnel dressed in traditional dresses with tablets of bratwurst and beer were welcomed by the guests. Tourists took many photos of the waitstaff with a background of the old city. It was a lively and friendly atmosphere! Eric was thoughtful. "I think Germany got back on its feet fairly quickly due to the American Marshall Plan for rebuilding Europe, and because the country supported the growing aggressive attitude of Russia toward American influence."

A beautiful trip via Ingolstadt toward Munich was especially scenic with beautiful and treed rolling hills, and neat towns and villages. The houses were mostly covered in red tiles and white stucco siding.

Eric turned to Louis. "How about staying at our bed-and-breakfast place near the city of Munich right here, Garching, as recommended. We can take another good look at our travel plans from Munich. I have some ideas I'd like to share with you about some literature I brought along." Louis was curious. "Well, I'm game if it makes sense to me."

The bus dropped them off at a double-storey green-and-white stuccoed bed and breakfast, one of several similar-looking B&B places around. A friendly reception offered light meals and drinks, and there was a restaurant close by.

A CHANGE IN PLANS

They booked a two-day stay, and organized their luggage in their room. "Let's go to the restaurant," Louis suggested. Eric laid out some maps and sheets of information. "Do you remember the American student I met in the US when we went there for meetings?" Louis nodded. "Well, I took along some of the e-mails he sent me later. I mentioned our trip to Europe to him. At first, I thought it would not fit into our travel plans, but now I have second thoughts. Our plans call for Austria next, then Italy, Greece, then back to Frankfurt for the flight back." Louis was getting very curious. "How about we travel from here by bus to Innsbruck, the capital of Tyrol and a very popular tourist town, and take a trip through the heart of Austria? We can stay there for a day or two, hike around. From there, we can go to Milano, Italy, the centre of the Northern Lombardi region. Lots to do there. They have many bed-and-breakfast places and youth hostels on the edge of the city, it says here. This is what the American student told me. He plans to travel to Basel, Switzerland, with a side trip to Northern Italy some time."

— 36 —

Lifting the Fog

"Hold on," Louis said, getting impatient. "That changes our plans to go to Greece, but then I don't mind skipping that for something very different. There are inner European problems in Greece that may affect tourists. I am not sure about Switzerland, even though I'd like to travel there. It's a beautiful Alpine country." Eric produced more literature showing Basel as a must-see for anyone interested in unique architecture, building structures, and educational facilities." OK, then, how do we get to Basel?" Louis showed interest. Eric spread out the map." From Milan, we can travel by train or bus, maybe two or three hours. From Basel, we take a bus to Frankfurt for our flight back, only about two hours, I think, looking at the map. We have two-and-a-half weeks to make the trip from Munich to Frankfurt. What do you think?" Louis wanted to know more about Basel and what they might see there.

Eric lined up the information about the project near Basel. "I think you may be interested in the history of that unique structure. It also mentions towns in Europe and other places connected with this city." Eric searched through his files. "I read something in this material that caught my interest." Eric settled in. "The First Goetheanum was one of seventeen buildings designed and supervised between 1908 and 1925 by Rudolf Steiner, an Austrian philosopher, author, social reformer, and architect. Steiner is one of very few major architects who was never the pupil of another major architect. Architects who have visited and praised the Goetheanum's

Siegfried Beckedorf

architecture include Henry van de Velde, Frank Lloyd Wright, Hans Scharoun, and Frank Gehry. This building was built of timber and concrete and burned down in 1922. The second Goethenum was begun in 1924 and wholly built of cast concrete and completed in 1928, after the architect's death. It was created with an unusual double-dome wooden structure over a curving concrete base. Stained glass windows added into the space. The ceiling's motifs depict the whole of human evolution. It houses a 1,000-seat auditorium, now the centre of an artistic community, with performers from around the world. Steiner also founded a number of schools. The first was known as the Waldorf school, which later developed into a worldwide school network with a total of 1,063 schools in sixty-one countries, as well as 2,000 Waldorf kindergartens."

Louis was fascinated. "I've heard little about Steiner. There are Waldorf schools in Calgary and Canada, I know, but I had no idea about his amazing achievements in so many fields. I can see your interest in visiting this place! Besides, I look forward to looking around the area. It is worth the trip."

Eric was very pleased about his friend's reaction. He had had some concern about following his ideas without Louis's interest or input. "I see here some flyers about what to do in Munich. We could take a tour of the city." Louis agreed. "I know Munich and Bavaria are being advertised as the most-visited places in Europe. Let's see what they are offering."

Lifting the Fog

The choices for sightseeing were great. Louis suggested including a visit and possibly lunch in the English Garden, as part of a city tour. A lively female guide explained in fluent English the itinerary of the six-hour bus tour through mainly downtown Munich, with lunch at the English Garden, also downtown. "Munich is rivalling Berlin as the most-visited city in Germany. It is the capital of Bavaria, the most prosperous state. The city was completely destroyed during WW II and rebuilt over many years to match its original, beautiful centuries-old architecture.

"Here we are passing the BMW towers and head-quarters and plants, a huge complex. The BMW Welt (World). Munich's Olympia Park is next. We are making a little detour to view the Nymphenburg Palace, with extensive baroque-style buildings started in 1664, and the former summer residence of the former rulers of Bavaria, the House of Wittelsbach. The German dynasty ruled Bavaria from 1180 to 1918. Its park and garden pavilions stretch out over 490 acres. Three hundred thousand visitors come here every year.

"The Hofbraeuhaus here in the centre of Munich is a very busy place most of the year. Next, we are passing the pedestrian zone of Marienplatz, one of the oldest gathering plazas. The English Garden, named after the English style of landscape garden-ing, is very popular with tourists and locals. It is one of the largest urban parks, even larger than New York's Central Park. We will park near the Japanese

Siegfried Beckedorf

Teahouse and Chinese Tower. There is a biergarten with where men in lederhosen play traditional German music. It's a good place to have bratwurst and beer. We have one hour to enjoy this place. Please don't wander off, you may miss the bus."

"What a place! Look at the sheep grazing way over there near the amphitheatre!" Louis couldn't believe his eyes. Masses of people walked by, and yet there were many tables available to sit and have a beer and some food. Visitors from Thailand were next to them talking fast and enjoying sauerkraut and sausages. Eric pointed at the sauerkraut and bockwurst on the menu, Louis preferred a bun and bratwurst with Munich beer. The German music made conversation difficult, especially as people joined in the singing. They would have liked to stay a while, but the driver made sure they would not get lost.

During the evening at their bed and breakfast, Louis and Eric got a lot of information about Innsbruck and its accommodations. There were bed-and-breakfast places on farms on the outskirts of the city of about 120,000 people, the capital of Tyrol. A train trip was the most economical way to get to Innsbruck. Both were happy about the tour of Munich. They decided to leave in the morning for Innsbruck.

ALPINE MAJESTY— INNSBRUCK

The trip to the main station gave Eric and Louis another look at the charming city of Munich, nestled in the foothills of the Alps. In general, people there seemed to be happy in their activities. The connection for the train ride was available within a couple of hours. There were no delays at the border to Austria. The speed of the train allowed sightseeing of the rising altitude of beautiful alpine country. Arriving in the late afternoon, they were lucky to have a bus connection to the Natters area with Innsbruck. The driver advised on the location of one of several bed-and-breakfast places on nearby farms. He stopped at the first one and they were lucky to be able to book a couple of days. He mentioned that there were regular bus connections to downtown Innsbruck. What a view! "Look at the green meadows, the snow-capped mountains." Eric pointed at the wide expanse "This is a picture book!" Eric and Louis took in this scene while a young man with what looked like a traditional Tyrolean hat approached from the large farm house along the road. No lederhosen, but blue jeans!

The young man spoke with a strong dialect and Eric and Louis could not understand a single word. Then he switched to understandable English. "Willkommen, welcome. I am the son of the house." He took both bags and marched toward the steep-roofed, alpine-style building and large barn along the road. After dropping off the bags at an attached building with two suites, he took the guests to what he called a common eating area in the main house under the same roof. Eric and Louis were impressed.

"A beer or coffee?" Beer, please, was the answer. "My mother will be along shortly to offer you some food. Are you Americans?" Louis explained the background of their travels. "Oh, I like Canada!" He told them that he was gradually taking over the farm from his parents. "We have large meadows and 250 head of cattle, some milk cows, and a few horses. A tractor gets me around to look after growing and making hay, and horses help me to check on the cattle. It was a good year! Cattle prices are high—a good time to sell." Now his mother stepped in and greeted them with strong handshakes. "My son needs to find a wife to help him run the farm." Her English was fairly good. "Mom, come on. I am taking my time." He was embarrassed, but his mother carried on. "I know he's getting close, but young people these days don't want to tie themselves down too soon. My husband does not want to retire.

Lifting the Fog

We would need to hire help and my husband is not giving up.

"I worked in hotels before I got married and learned some English. Where are you from?" Eric explained. "Now, let me know what you like to eat. We offer three meals, unless you travel around all day. We have sandwiches or we can get you something hot." Louis looked at Eric. "I am fine with a sandwich with my beer." Eric nodded his approval.

They were left alone for a while. Eric was quite happy with their choice. "We can look around the farm, maybe even help with some chores."

"How about taking a bus to Innsbruck tomorrow do some sightseeing and then sticking around the farm for a day or two?"

"Sounds good." Eric offered a "*Prost!*" to Louis. The father came in. A healthy-looking individual, he took his Tyrolean hat off and revealed a face sunburned everywhere but at the top of his forehead. His handshake was very strong. "I hear you are Canadian students checking out Europe. I am glad you found our farm. I think we are very fortunate to live in this paradise." His English was also quite good.

"A beautiful spot, as I could see when we arrived! You probably have a lot of tourists here in Innsbruck, but still live a peaceful life here!" Eric was impressed with his healthy appearance.

"Where do you go from here?" The son was curious. Louis answered. "We want to travel to Milan to get to know the northern part of Italy, which is so popular with Canadians. From there, we'll go to Basel for a few days before returning to Canada via Frankfurt. We will see a good part of the Alpine scenery in contrast to the northern part of Europe."

"Milan is a good choice," the mother added. "I worked there in the hotel business and in Munich before I met my husband. Milan is really a prosperous place—the most prosperous of all Italian cities—and beautiful to visit."

Sandwiches were served with another beer. What hospitality, what nice people. Eric and Louis showed their pleasure. The mother said, "Our farm chores start at six a.m., breakfast is available from 7-9 a.m., cafeteria-style. There is nobody in the second suite at this time. I need to know in the morning if you plan to be around for lunch and supper. I hear you may want to stay for two days. Let us know if you want to stay longer. The men have left, so you may want to spend time here or in the lobby by the suites. A bus is coming by here at 8 a.m. and another at 11 a.m., also returning from Innsbruck two times a day. It is only a thirty-minute bus ride, including several stops along the way. You may also walk around the farm, or hike to the nearest forest, about two kilometres away. There is a small coffee shop close by there. Helping out on the farm is not allowed for insurance purposes. Let us know if we can help with your travel connections to Milan and accommodation. We want you to have a good time here and send others this way. Have a good night."

Lifting the Fog

Eric and Louis were now well informed and expressed their gratitude for such great hospitality. "Let's spend a little time planning the rest of our trip," Louis said to Eric. "We are about a third through our three weeks, and we need to do our budget." Eric agreed.

They came to the following conclusion: to stay around the farm for three more days, spend three days in Milan, and to allow time in Basel and get a feel of Switzerland. "We have about one week, if we feel likeit. That amounts to our three planned weeks," Eric said, and assured Louis that this plan would fit his budget. Louis added, "I am surprised—we saved some money along the way."

After breakfast and talking to the mother, they decided to go for an all-day hike and return for supper by 7 p.m. "I can pack a sandwich for you to take along," the mother said. "And you may want to stop at the coffee shop, which has a little restaurant, as well."

Great view, fresh air, and sunshine made their hike a wonderful change to their travelling. "Louis, let's look, really look. This is quite an experience . . . a moment to cherish!" Eric stopped in his tracks. Louis joined in: "And let's smell the flowers."

They followed a sandy trail along the farmer's meadows. Father and son, on their tractor, waved at the two. They waved back, and Louis took a photo of the farmers. After some time, with the trail climbing, they looked at a dark stretch of spruce trees with snow-capped mountains in the background.

— 45 —

Siegfried Beckedorf

Louis and Eric started to feel the effects of constant climbing, and sat down on a log bench by the trail. "Deep breathing feels good," Eric said. "Yeah," Louis agreed. Looking around, Louis expressed his surprise. "This country is hardly touched by the world-famous ski resorts around Innsbruck. I mean, no residential density. I hope our hosts' lifestyle is not going to change in their lifetime. Let's find out what is beyond this forest. I am curious." Eric got up and stretched himself. The trail led through very tall spruce trees and, all of a sudden, opened up to allow a view of a mixed forest and Alpine meadows with clumps of willow. "Look," Louis said, pointing at a group of cabins and a store-like large cabin that were coming into view. "This must be the coffee shop they were talking about."

A sign displayed a "Hikers' Paradise Willkommen" on the front of the cabin. Louis took a photo. What a background! They checked it out and had their sandwiches with a beer. A bearded, elderly person with the traditional hat and long lederhosen, smiling broadly, said, "German or what?" Eric replied, "No, Canadians." "*Prost*, Canada. I know Calgary," he said in broken English." I was in Calgary for the Calgary Stampede—I think 1988—but not for the Olympics." "Right, we are from Calgary." Eric was excited. Louis wanted to have a photo in front of this place with him. He agreed, but asked to have their beer first. Now the two had to explain their trip, with the shining eyes of the bearded guy telling them how much he enjoyed the stampede, the show of the

— 46 —

Lifting the Fog

ponies and cowboys, and the great mountains. He had travelled around Calgary with some Austrian friends, including Hans Gmoser of skiing fame, who lives there! Eric confirmed knowing of him.

A free beer came along with the owner joining them. He kept talking about the stampede, the chuckwagon races, the dancing in the streets, the cowgirls in their outfits, and the pancakes that were served in the streets. "You guys really show the Western spirit." After Louis took the photo, he showed them a round trip following the sandy trails and leading to a shortcut downhill to the farm. "At one point, you will be on a plateau from which you can see the towers of Innsbruck..

They made it back before 7 p.m. and told their story to all three gathered at the table. "What a small world!" the father said. "This reminds me that I watched the Olympics on TV at that time. The volunteers really made the Olympics successful."

"Yes," Eric explained. "The facilities were expanded, as well as the downhill runs. Today, Calgary Olympic Park is still very active and successful in training and competition for winter Olympic sports." The son was surprised "This is amazing considering that most other places get into financial trouble after the games."

The next morning, Louis and Eric were ready when the bus arrived for the trip into downtown Innsbruck. The mother advised them to visit the old city centre, within walking distance from the bus stop. There is a lot of historic information there.

Eric was impressed by the amazing and ancient architecture still in good shape. In the museum, Louis could not believe the history of old skis on display (old boards, as they were called), so primitive and yet so heavy, and safe for the hunters and military skiers of hundreds of years ago. The information leaflets gave them ideas around what to do not far from the old homestead where they were staying. For instance, a display of ski huts used in the early history of the settlers spread out in far off and inhospitable locations of the mountains around. A sort of museum they could reach by bus. They decided to do that next morning.

The bus the next day went only two stops before letting them off at a place from which they could walk to a sort of museum, a collection of old huts that had been reassembled from far-off locations and were not in good shape. Still, each hut was secured with logs and otherwise left in its original state. They represented old structures with roofs of boards supporting mud and branches to withstand snowstorms and very cold temperatures. "They probably used whatever materials were available at the site," Eric commented, then added jokingly, "No architectural skills required." Each one had its own history and dramas. How people in those days could get around remains an open question. Some showed rough tools like wooden hoes and rough steel rakes, eaten by rust. They hiked around the museum, which apparently had also been a homestead with some inhabitable structures and an old sawmill.

Lifting the Fog

Louis had to take some photos, which he called, "The most wanted, please report."

At suppertime, they learned that that old museum had never gotten off the ground for tourist purposes, and that "you guys have a story to tell In Canada." Louis and Eric thanked the family for their generosity and hospitality, and told them that they planned to leave the next morning for the rail station in Innsbruck to travel to Milano. The mother wrote down some addresses for accommodation and sightseeing. "The train to Basel will stop at Lugano, a beautiful lake resort that's a mix of Italian and Swiss culture."

The train crossed the border to South Tyrol, an autonomous Italian province that had been created in 1948 and was part of the Habsburg Empire until 1918. It was a scenic northern Lombardi region before reaching the Milan area with green valleys and ski huts scattered along the snow-capped Dolomites mountain ranges at an altitude of up to 3,300 metres.

MILAN—ITALIAN HOSPITALITY AND ROMANCE

Milano is a metropolis of the northern Lombardi region, its financial hub and the global centre of fashion and design.

A taxi driver took them to a bed and breakfast near the centre of the city. Eric was curious about Milan. The driver explained that it's a very active and business-minded place in comparison to Rome and Palermo, where driving taxis, was "sleepy in comparison."

They had been referred to a house with balconies full of flowers. When they got there, they dropped their luggage in a large room with the help of a young lady. Again, the question "Germans?" came up and, again, Louis explained. The lady was surprised and said in fluent English, "Breakfast is in this room from 7 to 9 a.m. There are tourist information booklets here. There is a restaurant across the street."

Lifting the Fog

Louis and Eric enjoyed a pizza and a glass of wine while checking out the tourist information. Then they took a walk around a few blocks with a street map in hand. Eric suggested they take a tour by foot in the morning. Louis was impressed with the nice bungalows on the tree-lined streets and all the flowers. The sun was going down. To explore this city of 1.2-million people they looked at the literature for the city's hop-on/hop-off tour, an all-day sightseeing expedition offering many tours. They agreed that this double-decker bus was really the best deal.

A very attentive and pretty woman named Clara advised them to get there early. "It is only three blocks to walk." Back in their room, Louis ventured to tell Eric, "I'd like to have Clara be our tour guide from here on." Teasingly, Eric replied, "She has a nice personality. Why don't you ask her?"

"And then what if she makes an offer?"

Now Eric was really amused. "Then we'd have to part and you'd take her back to Canada. I will find my way. But check your wallet first!"

Louis contemplated an answer dreamingly. "Well, I'll have to sleep over that situation—if I can sleep."

"I respect your wishes, my friend." Eric sounded rather like a father speaking.

The next morning, Louis hardly had the courage to say good morning to Clara, he was embarrassed. Eric encouraged him. "Let's not miss the hop-along bus." Now recovered, Louis replied, "You mean the hop-on/hop-off." They got the seats at the front of

— 51 —

the top level. "We are driving by Milan landmarks," the tour guide explained."Here is the La Scala opera house, followed by the Milan Duomo (Cathedral), and the fourteenth-century Castello Sforzesco. Look at the skyscrapers of Palazzo Lombardia and the Porta Venecia, the historic city gates. We now see the massive San Siro soccer stadium."

For those of you who want to explore some shopping opportunities, you may get off and carry on later with any other hop-on/hop-off bus, or you could stay on for a short, refreshing drink or snack. "Why don't we take another bus with our tickets and walk to another bus stop?" Louis suggested. A huge shopping centre allowed them some sightseeing and walking around. A street restaurant with available seats was a good spot to relax. Milan appeared a pretty place with a long history with Rome and with France during the Napoleon time. "There's more of a relaxed atmosphere here than in Paris or Berlin," Eric said. Pointing at his street map, Eric asked someone how far it was from there to their bed and breakfast. In good English, a woman replied that it would be about an hour if they follow the main streets. They decided they'd be better off taking the bus. "Unless we play a trick with the bus company and walk!" Eric joked. Louis hesitated then laughed.

They found out that taking a certain bus would deliver them, with a few stops, at their place. This trip took them by Fortress Milan from the sixth century followed by the Main Square and the train station.

Lifting the Fog

Both were happy with their choice. Eric suggested that Louis ask Clara for another idea, like a park to take the bus to the next day for some greenery. With some shyness, Louis did so. Clara was quite helpful. She got out a map of Parco Semione, a 116-acre park that was a favourite among tourists and locals. The bus trip, she told him, would take only thirty minutes. Louis thanked her with a smile and suggested she sit down and maybe have a glass of wine. "By the way, your name means clear or bright in English."

"That is what my parents told me," Clara said. "I think I have time. It is not that busy right now. I like this park.I grew up in Milan. My parents took me here often. One time, I told my parents that I wanted to work there when I grew up. It has many beautiful, landscaped gardens. It is a year-round beautiful spot."

Eric cut in. "How come you speak such good English?" She told him that her parents owned this business and this house. They had helped when she was small. Her mother liked the business a lot, and her dad had his own little business, which he was selling to retire. They had wanted her to learn the hotel business and so had sent her to a Zurich hotel school after high school for three years. She liked it, and had learned French, English. and German. English, she said, was easy to learn. Louis was surprised by how open she was. "Now you are helping your mom. You are doing well, as we know."

— 53 —

Siegfried Beckedorf

"Yes, for now, but that will change as my parents want to retire. What are you two planning from here? I know you are from Canada, and that you visited Paris, Berlin, and Munich, and then Austria and Milan?" "Switzerland," Eric replied. "In particular, Basel." Clara mentioned that she visited Basel often while in Zurich with a friend who used to be a teacher at the Waldorf School in Luzerne and had tried to get a job at the Goetheanum. Louis now was brave. "Clara, you could be our tour guide. Right, Eric?"

"Sure," was Eric's answer.

Clara laughed. "You would have to pay me a lot. I have to go now. Have fun in the park. I wish I could join you."

Eric was impressed. "I think she likes you." Louis was sad and happy at the same time. "She is so easy to talk to, so natural."

They spent the day in the huge park with its many attractions. Both enjoyed its English Garden look and many winding paths and lawns. There were signs of the Napoleonic period as well as a mini-coliseum from the Roman times, when the open-air entertainment of chariot races attracted big crowds. Formerly orchards, vegetable gardens, and a hunting reserve, the park had been carved out and landscaped around in 1893.

Back in the bed and breakfast, Clara greeted them and wanted to know how they had liked the park. Louis thanked her and, with a big smile, told her they'd really enjoyed it.

Lifting the Fog

Louis ventured to tell her about their plans. "We decided to leave for Basel via train in the morning. Even in Basel, you would be a good tour guide, I am sure." Clara laughed again. "I am not qualified for that. Besides, I have some responsibility to my parents to wait until they wind up the business. I'll see you in the morning."

Louis expressed his admiration for Clara, but also had reservations. Lost in his thoughts, he mumbled that she was like that to every one of her guests, a real friendly tourist promoter. "She likes you," Eric said with a smile, "but it probably will take some time to get to know her better. Maybe you want to stick around a little?"

"Are you serious?" Louis questioned.

"Sort of," Eric replied.

BASEL, SWITZERLAND, ON THE RIVER RHINE, BORDERED BY FRANCE AND GERMANY

Clara had travel plans via train to Basel ready with a brochure and times of departure and arrival. Looking at it, she could not resist sitting down with them while they were having breakfast. "You guys are a nice bunch. It would be tempting to travel with you, even though I've taken the train to Zurich many times. Maybe you'll get stuck in Basel and stick around Switzerland. Or are you in a hurry to get back home?" Louis was lost for words, but caught himself. "We look forward to seeing you around Switzerland, if we hang around for a while. It depends on my friend here." Now Eric got into the act. "I was the one who got Louis interested in Basel. I showed him some information about Rudolf Steiner that I'd gotten on a trip to the US. An amazing man, philosopher, and founder of Waldorf schools and kindergartens around the world." Clara

Lifting the Fog

nodded her head. Looking around to make sure she was not needed, she told them that she knew a lot about Steiner and his Goetheanum structure in Dornach near Basel. She and her girlfriend in Zurich had travelled to Basel, where she was trying to get a job. Steiner, she told them, had studied all the subjects they were involved in, like design, architecture, natural sciences, and biology, as well as environmental issues.

"You know so much, I am amazed." Louis was impressed and Eric even more. "I can see that a week or so in Basel or Dornach could keep us busy." Clara replied, "I'd like to hear from you later and have you share your experience with me and my friends who are interested. I know an understanding of his philosophy is of great value in my career in hotel management. I'll give you my e-mail address right now."

"That's great, Clara. I look forward to passing on our interpretation." Louis was highly grateful. Now Clara had to leave, leaving especially Louis in a trance. "I am holding my breath . . . and hanging onto this moment."

In no time, the train passed Lugano, the centre of the Italian part of Switzerland. Lugano Lake surrounded by beautiful alpine terrain was a sight not to forget! Many ski resorts along the train route to Basel gave evidence of Switzerland's worldwide reputation for winter sports.

Basel, a city on the Rhine River close to the country's borders with France and Germany, is the

Siegfried Beckedorf

gateway to the Jura mountains and the nearby cities of Zurich and Luzerne.

Clara suggested a short train ride from the rail station in Basel to Dornach, the location of the Goetheanum. She told them there were several bed and breakfasts in that town. Specifically, she recommended the Engli B & B, a fifteen-minute walk to the Goetheanum.

The two-storey house was a real surprise to the students. It offered about ten rooms, each including a small bathroom. A roofed-over large patio with access to a walking path led to a public area for extensive walks. A lobby off the entrance allowed for a lot of space for reading, TV-watching, and gathering. A billboard pointed out options for guests, such as meal times with a request to let the staff know of their evening choices. A spacious eating area was located next to a kitchen and utility area. After registering, Eric and Louis had time for a light supper.

Both Louis and Eric were pleased. The price was reasonable, considering they did not need a rental car to spend time at the Goetheanum. After a cafeteria-style breakfast with healthy and tasty choices attended by what looked like businesspeople and couples, Louis and Eric walked through a park-like setting of beautifully landscaped neighbourhoods toward the Goetheanum. There, its impressive dome structure was a true masterpiece of twentieth-century expressionist architecture, called so by art critic Michael Brennan.

Lifting the Fog

The Goetheanum is named after Johann Wolfgang von Goethe, the German author, poet, natural philosopher, and statesman, who was also called Germany's greatest man of letters. Steiner wrote two books about Goethe and worked as an editor at the Goethe archives in Weimar.

Eric and Louis did not expect the amazing, large, and highly informative layout in the Goetheanum's reception area. They were directed to a visitor area where tourists and employment seekers could make inquiries in many different languages. With about 300 employees, there were opportunities in many fields. A library section offered lectures, conferences, and an events calendar, as well as books and training programs for teachers and students interested in the world-famous Waldorf schools.

STEINER'S ANTHROPOSOPHY AND WALDORF EDUCATION

One section of the Goetheanum's library dealt with the major topic of "anthroposophy," which was mainly developed by Rudolf Steiner (1861-1925). Eric and Louis were overwhelmed by the volume of information available to visitors. Both agreed to summarize the information for their own essays as they had planned and others in the future. The summary follows:

"(1) It is born out of The Freedom of Philosophy, living at the core of anthroposophy. The knowledge of the nature of humans, human wisdom. (2) The movement was inaugurated by Rudolf Steiner to develop the faculty of cognition and the realization of spiritual reality. On this basis, anthroposophy strives to bridge the cleft that's developed since the Middle Ages among the sciences, arts,

— 60 —

Lifting the Fog

and religious strivings of man as the three main areas of human culture, and to build the foundation for a synthesis of them for the future. (3) Anthroposophy is also an impulse to nurture the life of the soul in the individual and in human society— meaning, among other things, to nurture the respect for and interest in others on a purely human basis, independent of their origin and views. The main organization for this is the Anthroposophical Society, which exists in the worldwide form of National Anthroposophical Societies. (4) While rooted in a philosophy of freedom and an impulse to nurture a purely human interest in other people, it also has possible practical implications on lives as in various "daughter movements" of anthroposophy, the most developed of these being biodynamic farming, and the Waldorf Schools."

Eric commented to others later as a matter of interest to many that anthroposophy is different from anthropology, which is taught in more than sixty courses at the University of Calgary as the scientific study of the origin and development of human beings and their societies, particularly so-called primitive societies.

Siegfried Beckedorf

"Waldorf education is based on an anthroposophical view and understanding of the human being—that is, as being a body, soul, and spirit. The education mirrors the basic stages of a child's development, from childhood to adulthood, which in general reflects the development of humanity through history from our origin, far back in the past up to the present. The development of that essence in every person that is independent of external appearance, by instilling in his or her pupils an understanding and place in the world, not primarily as members of any specific nation, ethnic group or race, but as members of humanity and world citizens. Thus, the Waldorf kindergarten cultivates and works in support of the preschool child's deep, inborn, natural attitude around, belief and trust in, and basic reverence for, the world as an interesting and good place to live.

In the lower grades in elementary school, this leads to more of an emphasis on using artistic elements in different forms—not primarily as a means of personal self-expression, but as a means to learn to understand and relate to the world, building an understanding for different subjects out of what is beautiful

Lifting the Fog

in the world in the broadest sense of the word.

In the upper grades and high school, this leads in steps to an ever-more-conscious cultivation of an observing, reflecting, and experimental scientific attitude of the world that focuses on building experience, thinking, and judgement. The goal of Waldorf and Rudolf Steiner education is to enable students, as fully as possible, to choose and, in freedom, to realize their individual paths through life as adults.

While anthroposophy forms the philosophical and theoretical basis of the teaching methods used in Waldorf schools and is reflected in the attitudes of many Waldorf teachers (along with the general structuring and orientation of Waldorf education during the different stages of development), anthroposophy is not taught as such in the overwhelming majority of Waldorf schools worldwide. If anthroposophy is taught in some form by an individual teacher, it is done against the basic Waldorf tradition and in complete contradiction of the intention of Waldorf education as expressed by Rudolf Steiner as the founder of Waldorf education.

— 63 —

Siegfried Beckedorf

The Goetheanum, which is located in Dornach (near Basel), Switzerland, is the world centre of the anthroposophical movement. The building was designed by Rudolf Steiner and named after Johann Wolfgang Goethe, the German poet and author he admired. It includes two performance halls (1,500 seats), a gallery and lecture spaces, a library, a bookstore, and administrative spaces for the Anthroposophical Society. Neighbouring buildings house the society's research and educational facilities. Conferences focusing on themes of general interest or directed toward teachers, farmers, doctors, therapists, and other professionals are held at the centre throughout the year. Both the present Goetheanum building and its precursor have been widely cited as masterpieces of modern architecture."

INTRODUCTION TO THE GOETHEANUM— A GROWING ROMANCE UNFOLDING

After Eric and Louis paid their entrance fee into the Goetheanum for the day, they were told an eighty-minute English-language architectural tour included the main auditorium and the exhibition room. It would start at 2 p.m., would be conducted in English, and was available for the reduced price of fifteen Swiss francs. Eric was very impressed. "Louis, I think a week is not enough to get to know this place."

"Do you have any other plans?" Louis smiled.

They were directed to the Speise Haus, an attached place to eat and rest. A large billboard there referred to Steiner's legacy, a network that was spreading across borders, and making a major contribution to humanity and to humans looking for a meaningful life. Some people were gathering for the tour. "After the tour, we will be able to find

Siegfried Beckedorf

our way to people we need to talk to. I am looking for some input into how this man was able to build such a facility," Eric said. He was very curious.

About fifteen people lined up in front of a young lady who introduced herself in English as Ursula, the tour guide. She handed out a brief description of Rudolf Steiner's past and his dedication to create such a centre for learning. Eric turned to Louis. "She is quite sure of herself. I wonder what she knows about architecture."

"And a good-looking guide, I must say. Her accent is German—well, probably Swiss-German," Louis said.

The tour included couples, and what seemed to be teachers and students. Eric said, "I like a small group so we can be close to the guide." Ursula started out. "This is an English-speaking tour. How many speak German?" A handful raised their hands. "We are looking at a large photo surrounded by a wooden frame on the concrete base of the first Goetheanum. Seventeen other buildings were designed and supervised by Rudolf Steiner between 1908 and 1925 are shown over here. The intent was a 'Gesamtkunstwerk,' the German word for the concept of 'the synthesis of diverse artistic media and sensory effects.' It was begun in 1913 to house the annual summer theatre events of the Anthroposophical Society. There is more descriptive material in the library section.

"Back to the first Goetheanum. Architects created the unusual double-dome wooden structure over a

Lifting the Fog

curving concrete base. Stained glass windows added colour to the space, painters decorated the ceilings with motifs depicting the whole human evolution, and sculptors carved huge column bases, capitals, and architraves with images of metamorphoses."

"Any questions?" Eric showed courage. "I understand this structure burned down."

"You are right. We will come to that next. Please don't hesitate to ask questions." A very friendly smile was returned by Eric.

"Already during construction, musicians, actors, and movement artists began performing a wide variety in a neighbouring workshop. When the Goetheanum hall was completed in 1919, these performances moved onto the stage located under the Goetheanum's smaller cupola. The auditorium was located under the larger cupola.

"Now back to your question," Ursula said, looking at Eric and smiling. "Indeed, this building was destroyed by arson on New Year's Eve into January 1, 1923—the same year Rudolf Steiner designed a building to replace the original. This building here," she went on, pointing to where we had come from," now known as the Second Goetheanum, was wholly built of cast concrete. Begun in 1924, the building was not completed until 1928, after Steiner's death. It represents a pioneering use of visible concrete in architecture and has been granted protected status as a Swiss national monument. Please follow me to the interior of the main structure to the open lecture spaces." On the way, Eric was close to Ursula, who

Siegfried Beckedorf

asked him, "Are you an architect?" Eric replied "I am a student in environmental design and architectural principles from Calgary, Canada."

"Interesting, environmental design was applied by Rudolf Steiner in twelve residential buildings and glass houses here around Dornach at a time when not many were concerned with the environment. I will give you information about that later, or you may contact me in the administrative centre. I work there during the week."

As people gathered around in a show-and-tell area in the lecture room, Ursula continued. "The present Goetheanum houses a thousand-seat auditorium, now the centre of an active music community incorporating performances of its in-house theatre as well as visiting performers from around the world. Full re-modeling of the central auditorium took place in the mid-1950s and again in the late 1990s. The stained-glass windows in this building date from Steiner's time; the painted ceiling and sculptural columns are contemporary replications or reinterpretations of those in the first Goetheanum. In the dedicated gallery, the building also houses a nine-metre high wooden sculpture, "the Representative of Humanity," by Edith Maryon and Rudolf Steiner.

"This concludes our general tour of the Goetheanum. We have special information for those of you who are interested in design and architectural principles."

Looking at Eric, she asked, "What is your name?"

"Eric," he said, almost embarrassed.

— 68 —

Lifting the Fog

"Eric, you may be interested in that along with your interest in environmental design. If anyone else is interested in architectural principles, please contact me at the administration for another hour tomorrow. I will be there during the week. Thank you very much for your interest." She greeted the enthusiastic applause by lifting her hands and offering a great smile.

"Well," Eric turned to Louis. "Would you like to join me?"

"Eric, this woman likes you. Yes, I will join you. I don't want to lose you." Ursula was busy looking after people gathered around her, so Eric and Louis settled down in a space where people were sitting, having coffee and checking out books. What a good design the building had, to give people a chance to check out books and literature in comfort adjacent to bookshelves. It was not long before Ursula approached them with some papers in her hand. "Here is some of the information, I think, Eric, you may be interested in." Eric got up and introduced Louis. "Please sit down if you have the time."

"I will. I'll have a coffee with you while watching customers. Tell me: What brought you here from Canada?"

Eric explained his connection with a friend in the States who was in the same field of studies. "When he learned I was travelling to Europe, he drew my attention to the Goetheanum and Steiner's work and philosophy. I persuaded Louis to include this in our itinerary, and he agreed. Well, I'll let him explain."

— 69 —

Smiling, Louis said, "I enjoyed your tour and the way you made it so informative. I am studying biological sciences. I know that Rudolf Steiner touches on biology in much of what I have read about him."

"Are you spending some time here in Dornach? If so, I will try to assist you in getting to know Rudolf Steiner and his work, interest in which is growing in many countries, especially with reference to his founding role in the concept of Waldorf Schools." Here, Eric had to cut in. "I believe your enthusiasm is drawing a lot of people here."

"Thank you, Eric. My mother was a teacher in a Waldorf School in Stuttgart, Germany, where we lived for a while. Excuse me, it is getting busy here. I hope to see you a little later and I will also finish my coffee."

Louis could not help but express his feelings. "You are right, Eric, she is not only sure of herself, as you were saying earlier, but she is taking an interest in your curiosity."

"I must admit, she is quite knowledgeable and convincing," Eric replied. "She also knows something about architecture, as she wants to make sure people also read the 'Architectural Principles' she left here for us."

"Do you think we allowed enough time for this place?" Louis looked at Eric "You know she wants us to get well acquainted with Rudolf Steiner, so we can spread the word. And she wants to get to know you better, too." Louis smiled at Eric. Eric was serious. "I look forward to meet with her as often as we can."

Lifting the Fog

"This will give me time to summarize what I learn here for Clara."

"Here we go. Let's plan our time accordingly. Look at these papers here. Not only principles, but also Steiner's designs for about twelve buildings, as well as twenty-three references to international write-ups about Steiner."

"This paper here," Eric read one paragraph to Louis, "refers to thirteen other buildings designed by Steiner, principally residences in and around Dornach, as well as purpose-built buildings like the Glass House which houses the Spiritual Sciences. There are twenty-three references to writers of books and journals."

Just then, Ursula arrived. "There are bicycles for rent here in Dornach, a popular way to get around. You Canadians are different. Our young people around here don't seem very interested in the world-famous Steiner architecture. It is refreshing for me to experience your interest." Eric tuned in. "If possible, I, and probably Louis, too, would like to attend a lecture on anthroposophy, which is so well advertised here. It's almost scary for me to undertake such a seemingly complex subject."

"I'd love to arrange a time as soon as possible. Let's talk about that tomorrow. I'll see you here around 4 p.m., OK?" With a heartwarming smile, Ursula waved goodbye, leaving two excited guys catching their breath.

A leisurely walk in their neighbourhood the next morning with the help of the map Ursula had provided made Eric curious. These comfortable, well-maintained homes had mostly been built after Steiner's involvement. "Look at this one, here. It looks sculptured, artistic, and yet modern, fitting into the neighbourhood. Steiner was probably trying to create a greater acceptance of his ideas on architecture. There's what looks like a school building or hall with lots of sculptures. The Glass House it refers to must be in a location further from this part of Dornach. I would like to take a bicycle tour to get a better idea. Besides, it would be fun." Eric showed his delight.

Talking to Ursula later, he said, "You know, on our walk this morning, I saw quite a few young people, girls and boys, gathering in groups. Instead of talking, they were using their electronic gadgets to communicate, probably texting or whatever. We have seen this in other countries here in Europe, as well. I thought this was only a bad habit in North America."

"I understand," Ursula replied. "I am aware of that, too." Now Louis piped in. "This is why I think changes are in the wind. Many young people, students, and teachers all over can make a contribution to bringing awareness to that."

"I hope you are right. It could prevent many well-qualified students and other young people from losing personal communication skills." Ursula was serious. "Now, let's plan what I can do for you to spend your time here as best as possible. This lecture will last an hour, including a question-and-answer

Lifting the Fog

period. The subject will be an introduction to anthroposophy in the first part, and then a brief talk about the Steiner/Waldorf schools and their reception in Europe and North America." Louis was excited. "With some understanding and 'putting that in my pipe and smoking it,' as they say in Western Canada . . ." Ursula interrupted: "You have a good sense of humour. You mean your native Canadians?"

"You are right."

Louis mentioned that his friend in Zurich was looking for training opportunities to become a Waldorf school teacher. "Well," Ursula replied, "I can certainly arrange the interviews she may want to make here, and I can inquire about accommodation if they want to spend extra time here."Now Eric got into the act. "That could potentially mean that we would be five people going for a bicycle tour some time as well, including you." Ursula smiled. "That could certainly be planned and would be a lot of fun—with some planning around the time frame. It may get crowded for the two of you, right?" Eric looked at Louis. "Who would have thought we would meet such exciting experiences here in Switzerland?" Louis cut in: "Hold your horses, Eric. One thing at a time." Ursula said to Louis, "That must be a cowboy talking.."

"We in Calgary are all sort of cowboys," Louis said.

The auditorium was quite crowded. Ursula had mentioned that lecture audiences were made up of people from all over, mainly Europe, North America, and Australia. Ursula was able to place Eric and

— 73 —

Louis near the front row. As the show began, she appeared on the stage, followed by a bearded, tall man. Ursula took the mic and announced, "My name is Ursula Steinberg. I am a facilitator in the Goetheanum. I would like to introdeuce Professor Dr. Rheindorf, a long-time and worldwide educator and lecturer of Rudolf Steiner's philosophy and the concept of the Steiner/Waldorf schools. Our subject today is a summary of anthroposophy in the first part followed by the history of Waldorf schools and its acceptance in Europe and North America, in the second. The lecture will be in English. More information about today's talk is available in the library section. There will be a period for questions and answers." She handed the microphone to Professor Rheindorf. "Thank you, Ursula. It is my pleasure to be here to talk to you about my favourite subjects." Ursula had mentioned to Eric and Louis before the lecture that a complete write-up of the talk would be available in the library any time after the lecture and, later, in the library.

Later over coffee, Eric lifted his cup to Louis. "Here is to Switzerland!" Louis followed suit. At this time, Ursula came by and asked Eric, "What are you *prosting*?" Courageously, Eric said, "to you and Switzerland. We are impressed, Ursula."

"Thank you. You are sweet. I was pleased with the day's talk. The questions were appropriate and challenging. Our professor is lively, not a boring professor. What did you think?" She turned to Eric.

Lifting the Fog

"I liked his no-nonsense approach, the way he stated his convictions with an attitude of looking forward to questions. In my opinion, the people were very curious."

"I wanted to be open to anything new, anything I had not heard before," said Louis. "I got that."

"It's great to hear that from both of you. It shows you are willing to absorb new ideas in philosophy and education. I hope you can return here soon. I would love it."

Absent-mindedly, Eric looked up from his paperwork. He said to Louis: "You know our time is limited. I want to know, and want your opinion: what would the cost of delaying our return be, and what would be involved?" Smiling, Louis said, "I think you are in love with Ursula, and I think she with you. Depending on how things develop with Clara, I may also want to stay a little longer. I miss her. At any rate, we can phone the airline and check things out in Calgary. Why not find out before we meet again with Ursula?"

"Let me do that right now. I will phone or send an e-mail to Air Canada in Frankfurt."

Ursula joined them for lunch as promised, all smiles. Eric turned to her with searching eyes. "Louis and I are considering delaying our return trip. I am waiting for a reply from Air Canada in Frankfurt." Ursula declared that that would be great. Eric got up and gave Ursula a hug and said "I think this is all a dream come true. I am so fortunate to have met you. Maybe this was in the stars."

Ursula said," We have astronomers on our staff who could find out."

"How long would it take them?" Eric was in seventh heaven.

Thoughtfully, Eric told Louis, "I understand that if my intention and energy are in tune with a best outcome possible, there is a strong likelihood things will evolve beyond my expectations."

"And so spoke the wise man," said Louis.

"I believe that."

"I am really happy for you," Louis said. "You deserve the love and appreciation you are getting from Ursula."

"Thank you. Louis. And I appreciate you being my friend. Without you, I would probably never have met Ursula. I mean it." Eric was serious. "I am also smelling the flowers."

"I am, too. And I see sparkles on the petals of the flowers, like diamonds everywhere around the plants."

"That is a moment to cherish, the power of now."

They wandered around the Goetheanum looking at various announcements and highlights of the most recent Waldorf school events around the world. Eric's attention was focused on an article about some Waldorf schools in the States losing some of their particular methods and special features in the education of children due to funding from govern-ment agencies. Rudolf Steiner had warned of such developments and encouraged private funding for Waldorf schools to maintain their unique qualities.

Lifting the Fog

Louis commented, "I can see that happening in some countries."

Walking around the Goetheanum with Louis, Eric pointed to a section labelled "Comments by Attendees of Lectures." Attending the lecture on anthroposophy, Eric said, "It comes to my mind, How would Steiner's work have been influenced by the digital age, robots, etc.? I believe he would not have been concerned and would have looked at robots and the internet as making more room for quality work, whether with routine jobs, medical professionals, teachers, etc. To finding more time to pay attention to quality, not so much to job losses, but more qualified people in demand." Louis liked that very much. "Highly interesting, considering that the digital age is upon us. Consider the situation fifty or sixty years from now."

Eric added, "As far as Steiner's philosophy is presented here, I believe he would consider the arrival of robots convenient to society, rather than a thread to consciousness and the human spirit."

Ursula appeared and Eric showed some curiosity. "Your name is also popular in Canada. I know in Latin it means "little female bear."

"Yes, I know, but I haven't scared anybody yet. I know *you guys* are not scared."

"I am only scared that you won't be here anymore when we come back. You are so good in what you do, they may transfer you around the world."

"Oh, Eric. Remember this place is world headquarters for Steiner and Waldorf schools."

Siegfried Beckedorf

"OK. I like you as well as your name." Eric had to blink his eyes. Ursula replied, "By now, I know that. My mother gave me that name because of the Swiss actress Ursula Andress. Do you know her?" They nodded. "I was born in Basel, my father is a Swiss-German engineer, my mother is of German background and a Waldorf teacher. They moved to Stuttgart when I was little. My father worked for Mercedes Benz and my mother had a good opportunity to take a teaching job in Stuttgart. That is also the place where Steiner opened the first Waldorf School in 1919."

In the morning, Ursula confirmed that the ladies from Zurich would be picked up and looked after. "Now, before you leave for Canada," she said, "I have to bring my records up to date on your background, which I have neglected to do. You, Eric, start out."

"My parents met in Calgary. My father is the grandson of a German immigrant to Texas. My mother is of British background, going back many generations to immigrants from Scotland. My father was transferred to Calgary when the oil business exploded there. Eventually, they became Canadian citizens. They enjoy their retirement in Calgary."

"And you, Louis?"

"My father and mother are old-time French Canadians. I was six years old when they moved from Montreal to Calgary. They both own their own businesses and are still very active in them."

Lifting the Fog

Ursula was informed that the two ladies had arrived. She asked Eric and Louis to reserve some seats in the Speise House.

Ursula led two women to their table, smiling. "I have the pleasure of being in the company of two young and aspiring ladies. Here they are." Eric and Louis got up, with Eric smiling and saying, "You are nice to allow us to be in this company, as well." Louis looked at Clara. "How about that? It is so nice to see you again."

"It turned out quite nicely," Clara said. "This is Sylvia Mona, the friend I met in Zurich."

"You look almost like twins," Louis said. "Nice meeting you, Sylvia." After they sat down, Ursula smiled and said that the Goetheanum could make their stay worthwhile. Louis suggested dinner with a glass of wine or "whatever the ladies wish."

Over dinner, Ursula mentioned that Sylvia would meet someone for an interview to explain her ideas around being there. Clara said that she would like to know more about ways for her to get acquainted with what the Goetheanum is all about. She had great expectations for a future in hotel management and was looking for encouragement. Eric and Louis let the girls spell out their ideas. Ursula explained Sylvia's interview and let her talk. "I have been here before, but never got to what I know now."

At last, Ursula summed everything up. "We've covered a lot of ground, fertile ground. I honestly believe the five of us can contribute a lot of spice' to food for thought in the lives of others." They all agreed and Eric set the pace, lifted his glass and offered a toast to all, starting with Ursula, who complied with a winning smile. "Thank you for a nice evening." Ursula got up and gave Eric a hug.

IN AWE ... AND CHERISH THE SOUNDS OF SINGING ON THE TRAIL

The next morning, they gathered around their rented bicycles. They admired Ursula's very sportive looking bike. "This thing is my favourite vehicle," Ursula said. "I will ride in front. We have to follow a single line on the path marked for bicycles only. I will head for a path through narrow trails in the neighbourhood toward a place for a break and refreshments, a gasthaus with a veranda and view of the mountains. I plan to be back in time for dinner tonight. So we can take our time and do some hiking around the gasthaus area toward more open terrain with the mountains in good view."Louis was very pleased. "Ursula, you are not only a good mentor, but also an excellent pathfinder."

"Happy trails," Eric said, to which Ursula replied, "Here come the cowboys."

"Yes, I should have brought my cowboy hat. I'll make sure I don't lose sight of you, our pathfinder." Eric bowed to Ursula.

"In Milan I didn't get many chances to ride a bike," Clara mentioned. "But I assure you I won't fall off."

"I will be behind you," Louis reassured.

The caravan got off to a good start. The terrain climbed slowly. Many other cyclists were on the path, either on their way to work, judging by their attire, or for pleasure. It was a beautiful sight with only a few clouds, and it wasn't too warm.

Ursula stopped a few times to make sure everybody was still in the saddle. The scenery was overwhelming, like a Swiss picture book! Eric turned to Ursula and said, "This is wonderful. I am enjoying this trip a lot. It makes me breathe consciously. I feel energy rising. This is my inner strength."

"I believe you. This is powerful. A natural way to feel in tune with nature."

"Cherish this moment," Clara added, and Louis smiled. "This is the way I see Switzerland described in travel magazines," he said.

Ursula took the reins "Another hour and we'll be in meadow country with a view and ski hills around. So, let's get back in the saddle." Eric laughed. "Yes, my cowgirl and commander-in chief." Sylvia said "Get ready to yodel!" and Louis asked, "Does the echo come back with an accent?"

"I'm sure," Syvlia said. "Just do it loud enough! You go ahead first—I need to practise."

Lifting the Fog

The gasthaus looked like a typical Alpine resort with huts, mountains in the background, and open spaces with long tables. Ursula suggested gathering around the table space and parking the bikes in the provided area. "We can sit down. Food will be brought to us." Louis got his little camera out for this occasion.

Over lunch, while Louis was engaged in a lively conversation with his two women, Eric talked to Ursula. "This scene reminds me of a bicycle trip I took with my parents when I was twelve years old. We stayed overnight at a nice camping ground in the mountains. There was a large, roofed-over, but open hall. It was a warm night, I remember, with open fires; a real nice atmosphere. People had gathered for some music and dancing. My mother grabbed my dad and they danced with a lot of people joining them. They had so much fun. My mother used to be a dancing instructor. She loved singing and music. I watched her even singing while dancing. She made sure I took dancing lessons. By the way, do you like dancing?"

Ursula had been listening with great interest. "As a matter of fact, I would ask you for a dance if they had the facilities here." Smiling, Eric said, "Really?" Ursula looked at him and said, "Really. I begin to think we have a lot in common. Do you sing, as well? I joined my mother many times when she was singing in the house doing whatever she was doing, but I never took it further. I wished we had more

— 83 —

time here to enjoy each other's company." Eric was moved. "I wish that, too."

Ursula leaned back. "As we discussed last night at dinner, you will be back here some time. I think you will, because you have the idea of enriching your studies with the help of Steiner's philosophy. And I believe we've become good friends in such a short time." Eric held her hand. "I know I will return!"

They were interrupted as waitresses in traditional dresses came to the table to take orders. There was Swiss cheese, Swiss bread, sliced ham, and smoked sausages, fresh vegetables, and, of course, beer from the tap served in typical Bavarian "steins," apple cider, water, coffee, and tea. "A rich selection, hard to choose" was Louis's reaction. Alpine music and songs filled the area, adding to a wonderful atmosphere.

Ursula suggested a little hike on foot after on marked trails with distances indicated." What do you think about hiking about two km with gradual climbing which will take us along flowering meadows and a nice viewpoint? Our bikes will be looked after." No objections. "We will have an easier hike downhill."

What a beautiful and scenic trail, lined with spruce trees and meadows. Deer grazing and eagles drawing circles. At the viewpoint, Ursula watched Eric looking toward the snow-capped mountains, seemingly in awe. She approached him "And smelling the meadow flowers?" He turned around and hugged her. "Let's cherish this moment, Ursula."

Lifting the Fog

Louis clicked the camera "You are on camera." He smiled and turned around to take a photo of Clara pointing at the mountains to Sylvia, and he called, "Cherish this moment."

Back at the resort, they gathered their bikes. Sitting in the saddle was a nice change. "I just remembered," Ursula said before they got on their bicycles. "I have a folder of some German, Swiss, and Austrian folk and hiking songs in my backpack. My mother carried these around with her on our hiking and biking trips. She liked singing and my father had a beautiful voice. I had a lot of fun singing along. We sang often on our trails. On the ride down, we could try to sing. I have a song sheet and would lead the way. I encourage you all to sing or hum along while sort of gliding downhill. How about that?"

"Let's try it!" Sylvia shouted. Clara liked the idea, as well. Eric said, "I've heard a lot of these Alpine songs. I like them and can follow their meaning. And I was told I can sing!"

Ursula got her sheet and sang the first song. "We could repeat the verse often or pick another one." Eric almost melted as she sang. Sylvia said, "I could ride behind you and sing, then the others could hear us better. I know this song."

Clara liked that. "Let's go, if we don't get anywhere, so what? It's fun either way."

"I want to be the last," Louis insisted. "I know Eric can sing and I can encourage others on the trail to join us singing." Ursula sang the first verse again, including the chorus. "This song was

Siegfried Beckedorf

translated from German into English. It is about "the Happy Wanderer."

"I love to go a-wandering along a mountain trail. And as go, I love to sing, my knapsack on my back. Valderi. Valdera. Valdera and Vale. Hahahahahaha. My knapsack on my back."

It goes onto the second of five verses: "I love to wander by the stream that dances to the sun. Joyously it calls to me, come and join my happy song."

"Let's leave it at that for now. There are many more to choose from." It had been a very good try, leaving some laughing along the way and catching their breath, but not giving up until they had to take a rest. By now, a few people had gathered and were singing along while resting. It was a beautiful scene on the trail.

SPICING DAY-TO-DAY LIFE WITH PHILOSOPHY

Unsaddling back in Dornach in the late afternoon, Clara said, "What a great experience!" with a great deal of excitement. Everybody thanked Ursula, who smiled while getting organized. "I am very happy, you guys. You are a great bunch! I suggest we meet tomorrow for lunch. In the meantime, I will check what lectures and tours are available. All of you may also want to spend some time browsing in the library for books, magazines, and literature of interest to you."

The next morning, they gathered at the library after breakfast, as Ursula had suggested the night before. "Please browse here. I will talk to you later here in the coffee area." This took the four of them some time. It was close to lunch when they walked to the Speise Haus. Eric turned to Ursula. "I looked for a book with called *The Freedom of Philosophy*, by Rudolf Steiner, with the subtitle 'Living at the core of anthroposophy.' It's not available, but could be ordered. I would like to do that."

— 87 —

Ursula said "I will find out if the supplier can get it here in time for you to take along." Louis added, "I read a reference to another book by Steiner: *Human and Cosmic Thought*, with a comment, 'What convinces us of the truth of a certain point of view?' It's not in stock either right now." Ursula replied, "It shows you two are on the right trail in taking Steiner seriously. I will also check on that one."

Sylvia showed her surprise. "You two are advanced in your classes, as I can see. I will try to catch up on Waldorf education." Turning to Ursula, she said, "In addition to the information I picked up when you introduced me to a Waldorf teacher, I got more information titled, 'Breaking down the Barriers to Learning.'" Ursula was impressed. "I see I have to give you all credit in my records! I know you will be back here soon."

Their conversation at lunch time was somewhat subdued due to the time limit. Eric said, "We have only one full day left here before we have to leave. I'd like to just walk around the Goetheanum tomorrow; Louis may want to join me. You ladies probably have other ideas. But for dinner, I invite you all again tomorrow night." Ursula had plans for the women at the Goetheanum during the next day.

At dinner, she arranged the seating such that Louis sat between Sarah and Sylvia, with Eric next to her. It was a lively conversation, with both parties exchanging stories. Eric and Ursula talked about how to best communicate between Calgary and the Goetheanum. They exchanged e-mails, telephones,

Lifting the Fog

and Facebooks. Eric pointed out that he planned to have the support of his closest colleagues in pursuit of constructive cooperation from the teachers. Ursula spelled out her objectives to support his efforts in any way possible. "You know, your work over there can be facilitated by contacting the Steiner Centre in Toronto. I have an information leaflet I'll leave with you. We here at the Goetheanum can add to what you learn from the Toronto centre. They may not precisely fit your expectations as related to your motivation."

Eric smiled. "I will contact you after I get in touch with Toronto. I am comfortable that you understand my motivation around what I'm sharing with others entering working life: to maintain our individuality with a freedom to be who we really are." Ursula was listening intensely. "Like the example Steiner is showing in his inspiration of Waldorf education. That motivation of yours I have sensed and understand."

"Ursula, that is one of the reasons I want to come back here. The other is you."

"Really?" Ursula smiled. Eric took her hands. "Really."

"I know, Eric. That is a nice challenge and something we can only solve here in person!"

"I am looking forward to that."

Louis got involved. "These women invited us two for a brief tour of Zurich. Clara already checked this out for the connection to Frankfurt. There is very little time to spare. The solution, as per Clara, is for us to have dinner, for you two to take a B &B place to stay overnight in Zurich, and to leave early in the morning for connection in Frankfurt to Calgary."

"What an efficient secretary you have in Clara!" Eric said. "You should invite her to travel with you to Calgary." Clara said, "I have other plans." Ursula got into the conversation. "I am jealous. Too bad I can't come along."

"I'm sorry, Ursula. I owe Louis to make some allowance for his preferences. After all, I persuaded him to join me to come to Dornach."

"I want to be involved in the travel arrangements when these two come back here again." Ursula smiled.

"Granted." Lots of hugs concluded the dinner with Eric being encouraged to kiss Ursula who "cherished the moment," as she told Eric. There was some applause by the others, and a side look by Louis to Clara who gave him another hug.

The side trip to Zurich allowed for a beautiful sightseeing tour of Zurich, a city of about 400,000 and a centre for global banking and finance. The pre-Medieval history of the Altstadt on both sides of the Limmat River was in itself a beautiful sight, with a view of snow-capped mountains. Narrow streets hadn't deterred heavy traffic or a growth in tourism. Eric and Louis said that they would like to spend more time in Zurich, and that it was a very interesting place. They parted with Clara and Sylvia, saying "thank you both, and *auf wiedersehen*."

A TRIP BACK TO CALGARY

The size and layout of the Frankfurt airport's facilities, with train connections within the airport, surprised them. Their check-in proceeded flawlessly and in accordance with their booking expectations, as did their timely connection to Calgary. When they were 30,000 feet in the air, Eric relaxed with "cherish this moment." Louis responded, "And looking into space."

With a new view and zest for getting back to work, Eric was excited to read an e-mail from Frank, his American friend from Denver. Frank was equally excited about the e-mail he'd received from Eric about his experiences in the Goetheanum. He mentioned that other Steiner centres outside of Dornach were not at par with the Goetheanum. Eric said, "Frank has plans to travel to Europe with his wife within six weeks and will stop over in Calgary for a better connection to Vienna. He said he wants to talk to us in this respect." Louis joined in the excitement.

A month later, Eric and Louis had checked out the Steiner Centre in Toronto and been impressed by its Waldorf programs. They knew that their own interest in Steiner's philosophy could not be met without participating in the organization's six-month training program. They conveyed this to Ursula, who responded that she felt this was a good option, but did not like the time frame that saw such a long stretch passing before they would return. Eric was quite sure of himself. "Louis, I will keep my time frame of about three months."

"You don't have to tell me," Louis replied. "I am also anxious to get back to Dornach, and to Zurich for that matter. But let us do our homework here first." Eric said, "I understand, my friend. We got ourselves nicely tangled up. Frank's visit here may give us more feedback." Frank and his wife stayed overnight on their flight to Vienna first and then took a leisurely car trip through the Alps to Dornach for a one-week stay to visit the Goetheanum. Frank introduced his wife, Anita, a Waldorf teacher in Denver and the inspiration for his interest in Rudolf Steiner's philosophy.

When they were in Calgary, Frank filled them in on the work that had taken place since their meeting in Denver the previous spring. His colleagues and a couple of their teachers had met several times to find a common base in their efforts for clarifying items they'd discussed at their meetings. "I tell you, Eric, we are getting somewhere. For instance, we assume there may be a sort of intimidation when students or others apply for a position with an overconfident attitude due to their knowledge of, or experience with, a Waldorf or similar philosophy. So, what we

Lifting the Fog

have come up with—but more work needs to be done on our student newsletters—is to not compromise on our motivation to maintain our individuality, to give more tools for at least raising curiosity among employers around the benefits that the employee could bring along, like more dedication and productivity at the workplace."

"That is very interesting. To achieve that, I feel, we need to fully understand Steiner's educational programs and to go at times beyond our five senses. You know what I mean?" Frank shook his head. Eric smiled. "Thanks to a very nice lady at the Goetheanum in an important position by the name of Ursula Steinberg, we got special attention and guidance." Frank appreciated Eric's explanation.

At dinner, Louis turned to Anita. "I met a friend during our trip to Milan. We met again in Dornach, where she brought along a friend who was highly interested in Waldorf education. Both were taken care of by Ursula Steinberg, the lady Eric mentioned earlier. We made reference to you and your Waldorf role."

Frank and Anita were delighted. Frank said, "We couldn't have a better introduction. Thanks a lot, you guys!"

"Ursula took us and the two ladies Louis mentioned on a day tour by bicycles to the outskirts of Dornach and close to the mountains," said Eric. "We stayed at the Engli Bed and Breakfast in Dornach. Here's a business card for the taxi driver in Dornach. You have only a fifteen-minute walk to the Goetheanum."

Siegfried Beckedorf

"If at all possible, we may stop by on our way back from Europe. Thanks for your input." Frank was enthusiastic. "Happy trails and *auf wiedersehen!*"

Eric and Louis came to the conclusion that a few plans had to be made for the remaining two months before their departure for Switzerland. For instance: How to interrupt their studies—possibly a year's leave of absence, and potentially getting credits for studies between universities; how to finance a year of giving up their rental accommodation for more costly accommodation in Switzerland (possibly through part-time work with an assurance of permits); and how a personal relationship could influence their stay in Switzerland.

"How unromantic," Eric commented on the position of the third point.

"How sure am I about my relationship with Clara?" Louis added.

"Let's plan on this basis, and let the dice roll," Eric replied.

"That sounds good, this sense of adventure. OK. Providence and nature's guidance will play ball with us unless we maintain our focus with a very positive attitude."

Eric was impressed. "Where did you pick that up?"

Louis replied, "In the pile of material of Steiner's reference to Goethe that I looked at when I was a bit curious about that man. I should study Goethe's books."

Both enjoyed relaxing in the evenings and reading. Louis got interested in the book he'd taken along on

— 94 —

Lifting the Fog

the trip to Europe, *Scientists Confront Creationism*, by Andrew Petto and Laurie Godfrey. It was a book that examined anti-evolutionism in America with sixteen brilliant essays from some of the most important advocates in this field with overwhelming evidence for evolution. He noted of special interest a quotation by Theodosius Dobzhansky: "Nothing in biology makes sense except in the light of evolution."

Eric concentrated on the other book he'd brought along to Europe by Fritjof Capra, a world-reknown Austrian physicist and author of *The Hidden Connections*: *A science for sustainable living*. A comment by *The Sunday Times* in London said, "Capra has forged an interesting book which challenges wisdom, provides insights into social and economic pitfalls, and offers some light at the end of the tunnel."

They met more frequently and firmed up their plans. "I have news from Ursula. She had a good time with Anita and Frank. Frank is very much on your line of thinking and will take good ideas back with him. She said it was very refreshing to exchange views with Anita. She is a dedicated teacher and really enjoys her work. Ursula also mentioned she misses me a lot."

Louis was a little sad, "Clara is heading for her last semester in her four-year training. She has been offered a position after she finishes in about two months to work as assistant manager in a small hotel in Luzern, south of Zurich, on the Vierwald

— 95 —

Staetter See, a busy tourist city about one hour by train. She hopes to see me before she moves. I know she is very ambitious and that worries me a little." Eric tried to cheer him up. "Listen, Louis, look forward to seeing her again and focusing on a happy *wiedersehen*." Eric did cheer him up. Louis replied, "You are right. It may bring changes, but as I said, changes are nothing to be afraid of."

Frank sent an e-mail reporting on their beautiful trip and eye-opening experiences in the Goetheanum. "Ursula spoke very highly of you and mentioned that young people with open minds are an asset for them. Eric, you and Louis seemed to be meeting their expectations. She is sure you, Eric, will find good opportunities for settling in their area. She also mentioned that she is in correspondence with Sylvia, who will come for another visit here shortly, whereas Clara seemed to be heading for employment in her field of training. Ursula mentioned that both had looked around in Zurich for employment opportunities for Louis, who had inquired about that. Zurich is the centre for research in biological sciences in Switzerland." Both Louis and Eric were impressed. "How much progress has been made in our efforts to impress students and teachers! This is what we need in Switzerland, to get some understanding of our ideas and support in expanding our vision."

Eric and Louis were ready for the trip back to Switzerland. Eric was able to get financial assistance from his parents while in Dornach. His principal

Lifting the Fog

even suggested that Eric would probably enrich colleagues in their studies. Louis was assured financial assistance for a certain period from his parents and relatives. As far as credits for his potential work with universities were concerned, that looked promising. But they'd both have to figure out work permits in Switzerland.

NEW OPPORTUNITIES

What a nice surprise to be greeted at the railway station by Ursula in the visitor's car! Louis stepped aside to give Ursula and Eric space to exchange hugs and kisses, but got a big hug from Ursula, too. She took them to the Engli Bed and Breakfast. "See you later at dinner, OK?" Another hug and a great "thank you" from both. Then Eric caught his breath.

A director of Goetheanum in charge of international relations joined them for dinner. Ursula introduced the guests as her friends from a previous visit. He initially spoke German with a strong Swiss accent to Ursula then changed over to a flawless English to address the guests. "I heard about your interest on your first visit. Welcome back. I will do my best to assist in your further work and studies here before you return to Canada. I made a visit to the Steiner Centre in Toronto only three months ago. I noticed that the staff has grown a lot in two years. We are spreading our wings, which means we have to recognize the different expectations of the public in different countries. Our principle teachings do not change, but we are open to new ideas to structuring

Lifting the Fog

our lectures and programs. I am sure Ursula is assisting you in many ways."

"Thank you. What I found very interesting is that these two are looking at Steiner's philosophy as a spice to their line of work and studies, and show a lot of motivation as how to inspire others. You met Frank and Anita from the States here briefly. They are in constant contact with each other to broaden their own understanding and share their findings with colleagues and teachers alike over there." A lively conversation followed about life in Canada. "Now, Ursula, we are already in your debt! I am looking forward to the time we will have together here," Eric said with conviction. With a great smile, Ursula said, "We have a lot to talk about. I am impressed with your research and the books you've been reading recently. I know you both are very motivated to participate in efforts to influence future employers. Work places in institutions, industry, and commerce need to be open to an understanding that better performance and productivity can be the result of new employees bringing them with them into their employment."

An e-mail from Clara shook Louis up. He read it to Eric. "My dear Louis. Who would have known the changes that have taken place since we saw each other last. I know I am ambitious, and I know I can go places in the hotel business. The job offer I received after I completed my training with excellent grades floored me, but also excited me. I am now in Luzerne. I was asked to bring along some of my belongings, since the job was available right away. I love the people employed here, the accommodation, and the perks. And not only that, I was told the chances here in Luzerne are great for moving up the ladder fairly quickly. I will miss you and Sylvia. I talked to Sylvia about the potential in Zurich for study possibilities at a large research centre. Zurich is a big place with many opportunities. I hope I will be seeing you after a while when I have to return to get more of my stuff that I could not get into my car. Cheers, Louis. I know you will like Zurich. Give Eric my best regards. Your friend, Clara."

Louis caught his breath. "I do not blame Clara for taking that opportunity. She is ambitious and would not, at this time, let our relationship jeopardize that opportunity. I'd like to make the choice for Zurich because of its huge natural-bio-research centre, and that involves checking out the city. I will e-mail Sylvia about the opportunities there as per Clara's suggestions." Sylvia's reply came quickly: "Dear Louis. I am missing Clara, too. I know she will move up in the hotel business. I look forward to seeimg you here in Zurich. I promised Clara that I will help you to make the appropriate decision. I will pick you up at the railway station. I'd like to see you as soon as possible. I have time restrictions after the weekend. The hotel where I am working part-time has bed-and-breakfast facilities. Please let me know as soon as possible. Thanks, Sylvia."

LOUIS OFF TO ZURICH

Eric and Louis were surprised. Loooking at Ursula, Louis said, "This will leave me out of your planning for now. I want to leave tomorrow and let you know how things are progressing." Ursula commented, "Zurich is an interesting place to live and work. It has beautiful parks and river frontages. My family lived there when I was a teenager. The city is known for its large research centres."

Ursula turned to Eric. "The plans I worked on I will keep open for Louis for a later time. I now have only one student under my wing and that I am not afraid of!"

"I am sure I will not disappoint the best teacher in town!" was Eric's reply.

Louis hugged Ursula. "Out of sight does not mean out of touch," he said. "Good night, you philosophers."

"Eric," said Ursula, "please see me after you see Louis off. Happy trails, Louis."

MY PARENTS WANT
TO MEET YOU

The next morning, Eric appeared in the library sitting room with Steiner's *The Freedom of Philosophy* in his hands. Ursula smiled. "Good boy. I'll see you for lunch." Eric smiled back. "And you get back to work."

The lunch meeting was dominated by two love-birds trying to get their thoughts organized. Eric said, "Ursula, I do not want to interrupt your work here. I suggest I go back to my place now to digest this book. I'd like to see you for dinner tonight, if you have time."

"OK, thanks."

Now Ursula focused on Eric's face. "I have to tell you my parents want to meet you. They are retired and back from a trip. They travel a lot and would like to invite us for dinner tomorrow night."

"Oh, I don't blame them for wanting to check out the guy taking up so much of their daughter's time. But what if they don't like what they see?"

"Eric, who is the boss? They live on the outskirts of Dornach. I'll pick you up at your place tomorrow

— 102 —

Lifting the Fog

in my car and take you there—whether you like it or not!" Smiling all along, Eric said, "Things are getting serious."

"Well, if you don't like them, there is still me to deal with."

Eric could not resist getting up to give her a hug. "I think I told you my mother used to be a Waldorf teacher. She started out in Stuttgart, where my dad was transferred by Mercedes. The Waldorf schools had their beginning in 1919 in Stuttgart. She influenced me to take Waldorf teacher training as well as standard philosophy courses. My interest at that time was business management on the advice of my dad. I added that to my training."

Eric was impressed. "No wonder you play an important role at the Goetheanum. And how fortunate I am to have met you. Let's meet for dinner tonight, if possible, and carry on our adventurous ideas."

"Life is an adventure for us to explore with some room for common sense," Ursula laughed.

In the evening, the Speise Haus had filled up and they were lucky to get a table, which happened to be next to a couple Ursula knew from her work at the Goetheanum. Ursula bent over to talk to Eric in a low voice "This man is an architect involved in giving lectures once in a while in Steiner's architectural principles." She introduced Eric and a little of his background. The man introduced himself and his wife. "My name is Toni Sylvano, and this is my wife

Siegfried Beckedorf

Gisela. Environmental design? How long are you staying here?"

Eric answered, "This is my second visit to this place. I had to come back to do more research on what the Goetheanum is all about."

"I will have another lecture here in about a month. Are you interested?" Eric turned to Ursula. "Yes, I am sure I can arrange that through Ursula. Ursula introduced me on my previous visit to a lecture on anthroposophy, and I became quite curious." Ursula took over. "Eric is just getting started. I'm sure I can look after that and register Eric."

"Do you mind we join you at your table?" Toni asked. Eric got up and rearranged the chairs.

Toni explained that his interest was aroused in Milan where he worked as an architect. His firm had gotten involved in a project in which Steiner's principles were of interest to the contractor. "From there, my way led to the Goetheanum. We are quite busy implementing Steiner's ideas, especially where sculptures are involved." Their conversation jumped to the international attention that was growing in many countries. Ursula and Eric didn't have a chance to discuss their personal adventures, but had a lively time.

Eric saw Ursula around noon the next day to tell her he'd taken a long walk through Dornach. Ursula replied, "To build courage to meet my parents tonight?" and Eric smiled. "That may have had something to do with it."

Lifting the Fog

"Great, so I pick you up at your place around 5:30 p.m. Relax. My parents are quite casual in their lifestyle."

"I won't run away. I will be in the lobby. Thank you."

"Lebenskuenstler." Ursula said.

"What does that mean?"

"You are an artist in the way you express yourself and live."

Ursula laughed. "Really?"

Eric bent forward and hugged her. "Really, I mean it."

Eric was carrying a bottle of wine. When she noticed it Ursula said, "They like wine." During the car ride to her parents', Eric said, "Your dad is Swiss and your mother German. So they speak German at home?"

"Yes," Ursula replied. "My father speaks with a strong Swiss accent and my mother German with a sort of Swabian accent, because she grew up in Stuttgart. We lived there for quite some time. They like hiking and backpacking, as well as taking cruises. Mother always sings on hiking trips. This has slowed down somewhat due to their age—they are both in their late seventies." Eric had loved it very much when they had sung on their bicycling trip, and he told her so. "I noticed, and I loved it when you had a chance to sing along. You have a good voice."

"Thank you." They arrived and were greeted at the door.

— 105 —

Siegfried Beckedorf

After a firm handshake and hugs, they were led into the living room. "My name is Herbert—call me Herb. Brigitta, Ursula's mother, greeted Eric with call me Gita, short for Brigitta. Eric handed her the bottle of wine "Thank you for the invitation."

Herb started out with "I hear you returned here for a second time to expand your knowledge of Steiner's philosophy."

Eric replied with a straight answer. "You are right, but I also had to come back because of your daughter." Now Gita smiled. "We know Ursula is very impressed with your deep interest in Steiner's work. She told us about your involvement in Waldorf education."

"This interest is growing in Canada and the US," Eric said. "As a matter of fact, a colleague of mine in the US made me aware of Waldorf and Steiner. When I told him that my friend Louis and I had decided to travel to Europe to take a little distance from our studies, he sent me some information about the Goetheanum. A trip to Switzerland was originally not in our plans. When we were in Munich, I think, there must have been waves of energy traveling to turn my attention to the literature of Steiner, and probably Ursula's presence here was the cause." He turned to Ursula who smiled and replied, "Mom and Dad, Eric's sense of humour plus the fact that he can sing led me to like this guy so much." Ursula's parents joined in with her hearty laugh.

Herb asked Eric questions about Calgary while Gita excused herself to turn to dinner preparations

Lifting the Fog

with Ursula's help. "The first I heard about Calgary was the Olympics, I believe in 1988. You guys made quite some waves showing the world how to run Olympics without going broke afterward. It was the participation of a huge number of volunteers."

"Right," Eric replied. "Today, the Olympic facilities have been added to, modernized, and are attracting competition in winter sports." The ladies arrived and Herb lifted his glass. "Cheers to the Canadians, especially this guy, and good health to all of us."

Ursula carried on. "Mom and Dad, Eric explained to me his interest in learning from Steiner's philosophy. This is where I can help him and his friend Louis. Many students, and young people in general, are becoming aware of a lack of recognizing that the present educational programs in schools and universities are not allowing enough individual input and freedom in participating with teachers in the field of education. He knows now that the Waldorf school system offers good ideas. He and others are working on situations in which young people enter the workforce and, in many cases, are exposed to employers' indifference to, or even outright suspicion about, the Waldorf education. Possibly, employers are intimidated by their efforts to bring enthusiasm and creativity into their work and thereby potentially improving productivity and work habits. Do you follow my explanation, Eric, or do you want to put it in better words?"

Ursula turned to Eric who replied, "No, you put it well. I'd like to add that we are part of a growing

— 107 —

Siegfried Beckedorf

movement of young students, young people, and teachers, as well as some parents, in Canada and the US, who are trying to get teachers involved in our work. And we are making good progress."

Gita said, "Ursula may have explained that I was a Waldorf teacher for many years. We have similar problems in Europe—maybe not as pronounced; it is coming to the surface here." Herb raised another subject. "I worked for Mercedes for many years. They have good programs and pay well. But their management style is still the old style of "from the top down," like in many large corporations. There are signs of change, mainly initiated by younger people joining the company, but the older managers are uncomfortable with the idea of giving the younger generation more say in decision-making. They're afraid of losing their jobs. I didn't notice it initially, but I know it is coming."

Eric smiled. "This is what my friend Louis calls 'changes in the wind.' I know change is part of an evolutionary process. From the industrial revolution to dictatorship, traditional forms of business and all facets of social life are affected and we should not be afraid of it. Each one of us, individually, can contribute to positive and necessary changes."

Herb replied, "It is refreshing to listen to you. I can see you two, in my imagination, with you on the same wavelength, going on a speaking tour sometime to convey a message of hope and not being afraid of changes to come, whether we like them or not. And, in the process, waking up out of lethargy

Lifting the Fog

or a state of unconsciousness about what lies ahead. To being open to new ways of living and working. I wish you good luck."

"Thank you, Herb." Eric liked that comment. "That was good encouragement for the future and travelling with your daughter!"

Gita told Eric," I know the Goetheanum can assist you and your friend Louis in many ways. Ursula told me about Louis and admires your style of friendship."

"Thank you. We have healthy differences of opinion at times, but also a good sense of humour, which keeps us on our toes."

Their lively discussions continued beyond dinner, often spiced with humour. "I want to thank you, Mom and Dad, for a nice dinner and a nice time. I know Eric and I are looking forward to more dinners, something that I'd like to do at my place." "Or," Eric added," I'd like to invite you for dinner at some nice restaurant here in town, whenever it's convenient for you." They parted with hugs and best wishes.

Back in the car, Ursula said, "My parents really love you." Eric replied that he thought they wre great, and then said, with a show of affection, "And I love you very much." "Now Ursula stopped the car and turned to Eric. "How would you like to come to my place to top off such a nice evening with a glass of wine before I take you home?"

"I'd like that very much, a wonderful idea."

Ursula got busy getting her apartment organized with a comfortable seating arrangement and serving

— 109 —

wine. Eric admired Ursula's taste of furniture in her apartment. "That is you. I am holding my breath, Ursula, and cherishing this very moment." Ursula turned around. "And I love you," she said.

Their lively discussions spiced with good humour continued into the late evening. "Eric," Ursula suggested, as the evening progressed, "I think it would be a good idea if you stayed here. We've both had a few glasses of wine and I don't feel comfortable driving. I have an expandable couch for you to sleep comfortably."

"I agree. Besides, I'd love to stay here, and even more so if it's sharing the couch with you!" They embraced and lost all sense of time. In the morning, Ursula was woken up by the alarm clock. She turned it off, stretched, and put her arms around Eric. "It is wonderful to be with you." Eric joined in their embrace.

Ursula dropped Eric off at his place and asked him if they could meet for lunch. Eric said, "I will see you there. We have lots of things to talk about."

That was the case when they met for lunch the next day. "Eric, you made your and your colleagues' ideas quite clear to my parents, and I myself, understand now much better where I can be of help."

"So much the better as we understand each other on a personal level, as well, which I am very fortunate to experience. Let us carry on in this spirit. The way is open for you. As a matter of fact, Toni, the architect we met at dinner a few days ago, phoned and would like to meet with you in his office. His

Lifting the Fog

office is across the park on the other side of the Goetheanum and the park. Here is his number." Ursula was excited. "Who knows? He may have some good ideas for you, even possibly employment, part-time or whatever, in mind. Good luck."

GOOD SIGNS IN THE WIND

Eric met with Toni in the afternoon. Toni had been impressed by Eric's interest in Steiner's architectural designs and ideas. He told Eric of their contract with a firm in Munich to design and build an new museum apply creativity to Steiner's ideas and philosophy. "We have a tight timeframe with the city of Munich and would offer an opportunity for you to work with us for a while to suit your plans." Eric was delighted. "This would be an excellent opportunity for me and one of the reasons I came back here."

"We can offer you a flexible involvement suitable for you. I will discuss this, and a possible check-up with authorities about a working permit, with my partners . I will get back to you via Ursula, OK?" Eric was delighted. "I am looking forward to your call." Eric informed Ursula, who was very excited.

The next day for dinner, Eric read an e-mail from Louis. "Sylvia has been very helpful chauffeuring me around. As I said before, she not only looks like Clara, but she is as enthusiastic and lively as Clara. We have not heard from Clara in the meantime. On my trips around, Sylvia dropped me off at the UZH

— 112 —

Lifting the Fog

University of Zurich's science faculty, with courses in biochemistry and agriculture. I was informed of a field trip offered by large firm looking to recruit students and others in this field to join them. I registered, and had a wonderful and inspiring day trip into the country. After the end of the tour interviews had been held, I had a chance to talk to a representative of the firm. There is an excellent chance of my getting a short-term job on a flexible basis. There's no need to inquire for a working permit at this time. I will be visiting the firm early next week. Sylvia got me a small apartment on a monthly basis in the vicinity of her place. For now, I plan to stay here and keep you informed. Happy trails for both of you. Also, best wishes from Sylvia."

Ursula commented, "I am not surprised. Zurich offers a lot of opportunities." "I agree. Who knows what Louis winds up with?" Eric liked Louis's enthusiasm.

Toni the architect phoned back to let Eric know that he and a partner would like to meet with him at around 10 a.m. the next day in their office. Ursula confirmed the appointment on behalf of Eric. The meeting took place in a large office with plans spread out on large drawing tables. Eric was introduced to the junior partner, a local architect who travels between Munich and Dornach. They looked at photos of what the museum looked like before it was destroyed during WW II. It was left in ruins until the city advertised the site for development with the condition of rebuilding it to its original state. It was a

— 113 —

great challenge which Toni's firm was meeting with precision. Toni later remarked, "We want to ignore any straight-lined and right-angled structures, as you can see the centuries-old round features and sculptured little domes on this photo. To achieve that, we have to use wood as much as possible. Eric was fascinated. "Coming from Canada we, of course, don't look back to many historical structures. In the eastern part—Montreal, etcetera—we have old French historical structures, mainly churches."

Toni remarked, "I have been in Canada and was so amazed at the wide expanse of the country and how Canada functions from coast to coast, as varied and international in population as it is. It's a beautiful country.

"With your input, we may be able to bring the great variety of environmental conditions as they exist in Calgary to benefit our work in Munich. After all, the Chinook conditions in Calgary, I understand, are similar to Munich. I suggest you spend some time, if you can, with our junior partner, and we could meet afterward to talk about other matters."

Eric was very pleased. "I do have the time. I thank you for this opportunity."

Toni and Eric met shortly after. Toni laid out a proposed offer to Eric. "I discussed this with my other partners you will meet later. We have three contracts on our boards at this time—one in Munich, which has a pretty tight time frame; one in Strasbourg; and one in Milan. We can offer you a contract on the basis of no conflict with international employment

Lifting the Fog

regulations. It'll be for a minimum of three months, which can be extended, with local pay scales applying. We feel, in your particular case, we can offer four hours per day, flexible in that regard for potentially more hours. We would appreciate if you could be available within a week or ten days. We will have a written agreement for you to look into tomorrow, if you will."

"Toni, I am very fortunate to have met you and for the opportunity you are presenting. I have no fixed time program while here in Dornach. I'd love to actually work with Steiner's architectural principles and, at the same time, study his philosophy. All in all, what you are offering is an excellent opportunity to follow through with my plans. I also look forward to the lecture you will presenting soon. Ursula told me there is good interest and registered me." "Excellent, Eric. I look forward to working with you."

Eric could not wait to tell Ursula as they met for dinner. "Ursula, things are shaping up." He brought Ursula up to date on his meeting with Toni. "Eric," Ursula replied, "this opens the door to what I like to discuss with you as well. I have something I would like to share with you right along the lines of what you mentioned to my dad over dinner." I made some notes in this regard to not lose track of what I'd like to explore with you. For that reason, I'd like to invite you to my place for dinner the day after tomorrow." Eric became very curious. "I do not want to prod, but I look forward to dinner. I know this will be a highly

— 115 —

Siegfried Beckedorf

interesting subject, my dear Ursula. I can hardly wait." They hugged and kissed in anticipation.

A NEW CHAPTER TO EXPLORE AND EXPAND

"Ursula, I admire your unique ways, the way you prepare and cook, for instance. Here I am watching you to see how I can improve on my cooking talents." Ursula thanked him and pointed to the dishes. "I have here, wiener schnitzel with herb spices out of the vegetable garden in the flower pots on my balcony. There's an exotic sauce with a touch of paprika and barbequed baby potatoes. For dessert, it's rote gruetze, a grain-based pudding that's from my mother's recipe. *Guten appetit!*" Eric expressed his delight. He helped clean up the dishes before they settled down with a glass of wine.

Ursula was anxious to present her notes. "Now here is what I was referring to earlier. Rudolf Steiner wrote as a goal for higher grades, and as high school students, to enable them to freely choose, to realize their individual journey to adulthood. To ever more consciously cultivate an observing and experimental scientific attitude to the world. To build an understanding of what is true, based on personal experience, thinking, and judgment.

"I thought this statement in itself was a huge task for elementary and high school students growing up in homes where parents or society were in entirely different circumstances, unconscious of individual freedom or the potential for unfolding inherent qualities. In other words, students need to have a tool to generate a state of consciousness to open up to such a potential as early as possible. And parents need to change their own views to assist the young people. A tool for instance, I think, for even parents, just to pick from what you and Louis are demonstrating. To sort out what was put into your head earlier and maybe detrimental to your development."

Eric was surprised. "This approach could be an excellent example of what is helpful in a transition to Steiner's teaching—possibly also more effective in a personal and truly individual way on the road toward finding your true inner self before entering adult life or the workforce. Ursula, I think we have an excellent beginning here."

Eric continued. "Generally, what we—Louis, Frank, and others—want to do is raise an awareness, each one of us firstly individually, and then as the younger generation, to stress inborn qualities and freedom of participating in the educational process. I'm also aware that the younger people are side-tracked with electronic devices, which are often detrimental to their communication skills. Any changes, whatever they mean, are a challenge

Lifting the Fog

to embrace. I'm practising stopping in my tracks, becoming still, living in the moment. I know this is a challenge for many."

"Nicely put, Eric," Ursula added. "I suggest this is a start for each of us to put down our primary concerns and to, later, put our heads together. What do you see this collective approach looking like?"

"Exactly." Eric continued. "Louis, initially, mentioned appropriate articles in magazines, essays in student circulars, etc. Actually, we are attracting teachers and others' attention, as well." Eric, now fired up by Ursula's initial comments, said, "I am impressed and very encouraged for us to work together with individual input and original thinking, proceeding step by step. I think, once an individual asks himself the question, 'who am I?' the answer is most likely, 'I am the son or daughter of so or so,' as is commonly the case. This is the right answer until one day when— looking beyond what society is telling him—he may say 'I am a human being with a body and mind, but I am also conscious of being part of nature, its energy, its power. I am stardust-evolved with consciousness over eons of time.'

"Then, asked how do you know? The answer would be, When I breathe consciously, I feel energy rise. I let it flow from head to toe, through every fibre and cell of my body. This is what I consider my own power, my inner strength, in tune with nature.' I will discuss with you also a book by Gary Zukav, a look at an amazing reference to new physics and how this can affect an authentic power within us."

Siegfried Beckedorf

Ursula was amazed. "An interesting potential for our work to be even more meaningful."

"Now that I am trying to settle into life here in Dornach, I'd like to focus on improving my cooking and will invite you soon to have dinner at my place. Cheers to you, Ursula." Eric felt good.

"*Prosit*, Eric. I like our first evening of trying to find the meaning of life." Ursula lifted her glass. "How would you like to pull out the couch?" Eric embraced her. "I'd like that very much."

SETTLING INTO LIFE IN SWITZERLAND

Within three months of Eric's new responsibilities, he and Ursula had made good progress in their discussions regarding their ideas. Louis and Sylvia joined them during one weekend for lively talks and bicycle rides. Sylvia and Louis made no fuss about their closer relationship as Clara moved up into her career. Louis had committed to a steadier job position. Frank corresponded regularly about meetings with a growing circle of like-minded people.

Toni and Eric agreed to extend their working contract to a minimum of six months. In this negotiation, Eric mentioned that he planned to make a two week trip to Canada at some point soon. Toni told him that that was good timing for them.

A VISIT ACROSS THE POND

Ursula and Eric discussed a potential trip to Canada. "I'd like to take you along to have a look around and also to meet my parents." Initially, Ursula showed some concern about leave for a holiday without proper notice. Then she checked it out with her superiors and got the go-ahead. "I am excited! Let's get wheels in motion." They also passed this idea along to Louis, who replied, "I would enjoy that, but my job could be at risk. I am OK for now here and plan to travel later."

Eric booked a flight with Swiss Airlines directly to Vancouver with a connection to Calgary, so Ursula could see the West Coast and sightsee in Vancouver for two days. Coming in on the plane, Ursula said she was impressed with the city surrounded by snow-capped mountains and the Pacific Ocean. On arrival at the airport in Calgary, the very modern look and expanding size of the young city surprised her. They were met with hugs by Eric's parents, Ronny and Liz. Accommodation was arranged and a dinner

Lifting the Fog

prepared at their home. Ursula admired the view of the foothills and mountains in the background. "I was aware of Canada as a huge country, but seeing the wide expanse is amazing."

Ronny lifted his glass. "Let us toast to a welcome in Canada and good health to us all." Liz added with a lovely British accent that was in contrast to Ronny's touch of Texan slang, "Ursula, I am fortunate to meet you here with Eric." Ursula gave her another hug.

Of course, the conversation soon turned to one of the reasons for their Calgary trip. Eric mentioned their meeting with Frank and Anita from Denver in three days in Calgary and their connection to that couple. Eventually, talk moved to Ursula's work at the Goetheanum, as well as Eric's involvement in Steiner's architecture with a Dornach firm. Ronny, a bit surprised, said, "Well, does that mean you're moving to Switzerland?"

"Eventually, it may. Ursula and I have plans for the future, but as yet, they are not cast in stone." Liz turned to Ursula. "I understand you are also involved in the Waldorf education. I am a little acquainted with the Waldorf concept. We have a Waldorf school in our neighbourhood, and our neighbour's children have gone there for many years. They are very pleased with the effect on them."

Ronny was curious. "You have noble ideas. And who doesn't want changes in our educational systems? With many systems competing worldwide, there's a need for a system that pays attention to early childhood, starting with kindergarten. In addition, we all see young people at a loss when it comes to choosing a career and finding individual acceptance. But where do you start?"

"Each one of us, young or old, can start making a change in our own attitude," Eric replied. "There's another point on which I exchanged views with Frank before we left Switzerland: a growing concern about an addiction among young people aged ten to twenty. I'm referring to the digital tools, the smartphones, the TV shows, and the computer games. It's scientifically proven in many countries that the constant use of this technology for things other than schoolwork is produces a lack of concentration, a lack of initiative to learn, and a loss of communication skills.

"Here, again, parents and educators alike have to wake up. Within a few years, these developments may show up in educational standards seriously dropping. Ursula has also noticed this concern among grown-ups in our neighbourhood."

Ronny replied, "We all know the benefits of the internet in all facets of our lives. What you are talking about is the downside of the computer revolution. I'm concerned if this is not realized soon, it may be too late to stop or at least curtail it."

Liz turned to Ursula "The Waldorf concept, as I understand it, seems to deal with this as a distraction in learning."

"You are quite right," Ursula replied. "This is evident in much of the teachings of Rudolf

Lifting the Fog

Steiner. Hopefully, parents will begin to notice that eventually."

What a scenic tour for Ursula! A car trip to Lake Louise, Alberta, was an exciting experience with a view of the lake and glaciers. The town was only discovered by early explorers in the late 1880s during the planning process to build and close the link to British Columbia with the amazing Canadian Pacific Railway, from coast to coast. This location, known worldwide as Lake Louise, is one of the wonders of nature. A hike up the trails surrounding the lake added to the excitement and lunch at the Chateau of Lake Louise in the afternoon topped the experience.

The meeting with Frank and Anita from Denver extended over a full day, with some of Eric's former colleagues in attendance. An e-mail from Louis in Zurich added to a very productive meeting. In it, Louis elaborated on a report by a German news channel about the huge concern over nuclear energy, and the continued efforts by countries like the US, Japan, and France, to build atomic bombs. The location of the initial efforts for constructing the uranium and plutonium production facilities date back to the first years after WWII. In the meantime, these plants were being dismantled and decontaminated at the health risks of the remaining population in the affected areas. The population in general is employed in masses to keep them in place and quiet in the decontamination process. Concerns are now surfacing among citizens in the areas about proven radiation effects on families. No reference was made to the situation in countries governed by dictators, like North Korea, Russia, and China, or even Pakistan and India.

Louis added that, in his circle of like-minded people in Zurich, they're considering the idea of creating a student magazine covering concerns of this nature, along with what Eric, Ursula, and Frank had discussed about concerns that the digital age was upon us. The e-mail from Louis added considerable interest to the idea of proceeding with the student paper, expanding it first to the US, initiated by Frank and Anita. The process, Frank mentioned, would entail students, teachers, and principals in institutions where students were active in this respect. Eric's colleague in Calgary expressed interest in getting support for a similar action.

Anita prepared a report covering this meeting and its conclusion of notifying those concerned before Frank and Anita left for Denver. Ursula and Eric were pleased with their achievements and sent a copy of the report to Louis with the announcement that they would return as soon as Eric concluded some meetings with colleagues, designers, and architects in Calgary who'd expressed interest in Steiner's architectural principles. Both parties had great interest in straight-line architecture in the tall commercial office buildings constantly being added to the Calgary skyline, as well as in unique types of commercial and retail structures. Ideas were expressed and business cards exchanged.

Lifting the Fog

Ursula and Eric rented a car and spent a weekend in the Banff National Park for hiking and a good time in the colourful autumn atmosphere. On a plateau with a panoramic view of the snow-capped mountains, Eric stood in awe, holding his breath. Ursula said, "We are very fortunate, Eric, to be able to experience these moments."

Eric's parents invited them for another dinner before leaving for Switzerland. The conversation was dominated by Ronny's and Liz's interest in their discussion with Frank and Anita. Ronny was very interested. "Your concerns are real and it's worthwhile for you to seek a lot of attention for them." Liz added, "Maybe you can spread your efforts to London in the future. It would give you a chance to visit Britain."

Eric replied, "We talked about such a visit."

BACK IN THE SADDLE IN DORNACH

While Ursula was catching up with business in the Goetheanum, Eric was invited to accompany the junior partner and designer on trips to Milan and Strassbourg. Toni, in the meantime, was excited to receive an e-mail from one of the Calgary contacts confirming Eric and Ursula's meetings. A design exchange correspondence took place shortly after.

During dinner at Ursula's parents' place, Herb expressed surprise about the progress made in Calgary with the efforts by the like-minded groups in their meetings. Gita added, "Rudolf Steiner would probably have enjoyed being present at these meetings."

Ursula smiled. "Most likely."

LET THE BELLS RING

Within two months of their return from Calgary, Ursula told her parents that Eric and she had decided to get married in the next spring in Dornach. Great excitement followed, with Herb and Gita ready to help with preparations. Eric would credits for his studies in Switzerland while being employed by Toni's firm. "We are looking for a place to buy in the neighbourhood, as Eric feels comfortable settling in Dornach. He will notify his parents and invite them to come for the wedding. They may want to spend a holiday in Switzerland. So, my parents, Eric will take me off your attention, but not out of your sight."

Eric joined in. "This is in anticipation that I have your approval."

Ursula added, "With or without approval, but with a lot of love."

SWITZERLAND— HERE WE COME

Ursula emphasized to her parents that she and Eric preferred a small wedding with only the closest of relatives and friends in attendance. A guest list was prepared. No matter how much they kept the number down, about seventy people confirmed. Herb made arrangements for the event with the Dornach Community Hall. Guests from outside Switzerland and Europe combined their attendance with a holiday in Switzerland.

Ursula insisted on not wearing a special wedding dress, and chose a typical Swiss traditional dress. She looked very Swiss, very Alpine. She told her relatives and friends that she would be practising to yodel, but would not guarantee anything. Eric complemented her traditional attire with a "Western look." His choice not to include a cowboy hat "indicated a softening of his Western look." During the ceremony, Eric whispered into Ursula's ear, "Cherish this moment." In turn, Ursula squished his hand.

Lifting the Fog

She had requested a tango for the first dance and asked the guests to follow suit.

A great party followed, with Ursula's wish fulfilled to have typical German, Austrian, and Swiss songs played with the appropriately dressed band playing matching music. The community hall was made available for many of the guests the next day for continued visiting and getting acquainted. Ursula and Eric retreated in the early-morning hours for a week-long honeymoon.

A Tragic Accident

Within a year of the wedding and as Ursula and Eric were settling in their new home, a phone call from Ursula's father brought devastating news. Herb and Gita had suffered a severe car accident near Bern. Gita had been taken to the hospital in Bern by ambulance with life-threatening injuries. Herb had only suffered minor injuries.

Ursula and Eric consoled each other. Eric suggested driving to Bern in the morning after notifying Toni and the Goetheanum. Ursula agreed with such quick action and informed her dad, who was staying close to Gita in the emergency department.

Herb took them aside as they arrived and told them that Gita was conscious. To their relief, no head injuries were reported, but severe leg fractures, neck and internal injuries, and substantial blood loss made the situation serious. Eric and Ursula took turns with Herb to be close to Gita. They decided to take hotel accommodation for a few days.

Within twenty-four hours of the doctors' decision to transfer blood, the situation improved. Gita was able to move her neck, even though heavy bandages made that difficult. Ursula held her hand on her mom's cheek and smiled. Gita was able to return the smile, especially with her eyes. She looked at Eric and her husband with bright eyes—what a relief! Ursula decided to remain in Bern with her dad. They didn't expect Gita to be transferred to a hospital closer to home for a few weeks.

Herb suggested Eric drive back to Dornach. "I will take Ursula home within a week or so. By the way, Eric, when you drive back, take a side trip through the Altstadt of Bern, a historic town dating back to the twelfth century that has a lot of medieval buildings preserved in its Old Town. The Federal Place dates back to the thirteenth century." Eric was in awe about the condition and architecture displayed in the centre.

Two months later, Gita was able to be transferred to Basel. A wheelchair made it possible to move around should she could be with her family frequently. Her mental condition was considered to be quite optimistic and she was ready for regular physiotherapy. Herb commented, "I was told that Gita would not be able to be moved by car for quite some time, but I will get her home in a few months. We are fortunate to see her in this condition!"

CHANGES IN THE WIND

Within about ten years of Frank, Eric and Louis engaging in their first discussions about students' concerns around not being heard, regular attention was being drawn to the subject in student magazines in universities, high schools and colleges in the US, Canada, and Central Europe. Regular meetings between student groups, educators, and principals were being held to improve communication among these groups with astounding results. Parents, teachers, and students increasingly participation and showed interest in improving their immediate family and working lives, as well as their social, business and political affairs. Comments surfaced from many university teachers expressing interest in communication.

Frank, Eric, and Louis, as well as many other parties, were engaged regularly in providing student magazines with news and miscellaneous items referencing changes in the wind. Louis reported on a growing concern around a rise in "biopiracy," the patenting of plant life forms by large biotech corporations. Existing national laws and international conventions prohibit the patenting of essential natural resources, such as food. In recent years, health problems caused by genetic engineering—as well as deeper social, ecological, and ethical problems—have become all too apparent. There has been, for some time now, a growing global movement that rejects this form of technology. All these developments were of great interest to teachers, students, and others who normally would not be aware of them.

Eric contributed an article about positive developments taking place with reference to halting and reversing the present depletion of resources, pollution, extinction of species, and global climate change. He referred to Fritjof Capra's book, *Hidden Connections*, and quoted authors in the field of sustainable development.

Lester Brown: "I believe that there are now clear signs that the world does seem to be approaching a kind of paradigm shift in environmental consciousness. Across a spectrum of activities, places, and institutions, the atmosphere has changed markedly in just the last few years."

Amory Lovins: "I am more hopeful now than a few years ago. I think the speed and importance of things getting better, outweighs the speed and importance of things getting worse. One of the most hopeful developments is the co-operation between the North and the South in the global civil society. We have much richer expertise available now than we had before.

Lifting the Fog

Vandana Shiva: "I am optimistic, because life has its own ways of not becoming extinct; and people, too, have their own ways. They will continue life's tradition."

Eric added" When I passed this on to Frank, he commented that he feels the only drawback he can see is the lack of co-operation by politicians and governments leaning to dictatorship. I agree with Frank."

Ursula was instrumental in organizing lectures within the Goetheanum with speakers from the fields of philosophy, science, technology, the arts, and commerce. Preparations had been made some time before to put attention on the influence of philosophy in these fields of occupation. Eric commented to Ursula "You are carrying the flag beautifully."

Ursula, with a sheepish smile, said, "The time has come, my dear!"

Toni the architect delivered several lectures along these lines that were attended by architects and designers, as well as many others.

A VISIT FROM ZURICH

A visit by Louis and Sylvia to Dornach allowed for lively discussions with Ursula and Eric. Sylvia joined Louis in order to participate in lectures mentioned by Ursula. Both planned a visit to Calgary within a month. "Are you ready for another trip?" Louis asked Eric, who shook his head with a look at Ursula. "We don't have any plans at this time." Now Sylvia joined in, smiling. "We will follow in your steps and get married in Dornach after we get back from Canada."

"Yes," Louis beamed. "We feel very much at home in Zurich and wish you'd moved there, as well."

"This is how Eric and I feel about Dornach, but visiting you more frequently would be a good idea." Ursula gave Sylvia a hug. "What excitement lies ahead for you two!"

To Louis, Eric said, "Well, Louis you are now in for a beautiful 'change in the wind!' I wish you both a lot of happiness and a real nice trip!" Sylvia mentioned that they had a few days and that she'd like to attend one more lecture in Waldorf education while she was in Dornach in order to pursue her dream

Lifting the Fog

of getting into Waldorf education and leaving the hotel business. Louis and she thought a bicycle tour would be nice, and wondered if it could be arranged. Ursula confirmed that that depended on Eric's time, as well. "We have been bicycling a lot. I will arrange to join you," Eric replied.

Over dinner, the four exchanged their experiences and discussed the progress that had been made, including what Frank had detailed to Louis. Louis pointed out that he had to re-read several chapters of Steiner's book, *Human and Cosmic Thought*. "It was and still is difficult for me to comprehend Steiner's writings and lectures, even though he appreciates the variety of possible worldviews and tries to promote tolerance of other people's opinions." Ursula replied, "There are several lectures offered here in the Goetheanum during the year that deal with Steiner's 'quality of cosmic thought,' and require an open mind."

LIFTING THE FOG
WITH AWARENESS

Sylvia added to Louis's closing words: "Having been around you guys for some time now, I, too, have become somewhat philosophical in another way with reference to an open mind. I am keeping a journal about thoughts and ideas worth remembering. I have my little journal here in my purse, and I want to read a summary of something I wrote recently. When I told Louis, he said that it was the same thing he and Eric do frequently. 'To stop in our tracks and enjoy the moment.' Maybe that made me think about this. But I go a little further."

"I am questioning myself on what the first activity after I wake up is. It is breathing. Do I have to think to breathe? No. What is the difference between letting breathing happen and becoming aware of breathing?

I, myself, being aware of this moment, puts me in charge of the way I breathe and I am conscious of energy rising within my body. I let it flow into every cell. It feels good. Now my awareness turns to

Lifting the Fog

who I am. I am more than my body and mind; they are amazing tools, but who am I? We are all part of nature, its energy, its power. We evolved out of stardust with consciousness over eons of time. So tuning into this natural energy, I feel it rising when I breathe consciously. I feel one with the energy of nature, the universe. This, I know, is my own power."

Eric lined up first. "Wonderful. Sylvia. I have followed this exercise for some time. It is amazing how you arrived at this 'finding your own strength.'" He turned to Louis. "It is amazing even though we both talked about 'holding our breath.'

"Sylvia, you will find your inner strength with that exercise and it is so practical. In doing my breathing exercises, I am becoming aware of being consciousness—my consciousness, with habitual exercises holding together body and mind, watching and thinking about habits."

Ursula added, "Eric, that is food for thought. This is great, Sylvia! Seeing you as a Waldorf teacher soon, you will have an inner drive to offer an excellent wake-up call to your students." Louis, smiling at Sylvia, said, "How fortunate I am to have a partner to keep me aware and on my toes." Sylvia thanked them all. "I feel encouraged to share my way of finding strength and my own power with you and others."

IN AWE—CHERISHIING THE SOUNDS ON THE TRAILS AGAIN

The bicycling tour followed the same route as the one before. The four enthusiastic cyclers gathered again at the gasthaus for a lunch break. In no time, their singing—led by Ursula and melting Eric again—was joined in by others on a break. A hike further up the trail followed. This time it was Louis who was fascinated by the view from a plateau and joined by Sylvia in a state of awe. "Hold onto this moment!" Eric and Ursula joined in their excitement. Fired on by this experience, the four cycled back, singing and laughing. Unsaddling in Dornach, they were already planning their next get-together

AGAIN, WEDDING BELLS RING IN DORNACH

Three months later, Sylvia and Louis arrived for their wedding in Dornach. The ceremony also took place in the Dornach Community Hall, and almost the same people attended as did for Ursula's and Eric's celebration. Clara was invited, as well.

Ursula and Eric joined the newly married couple a week later in the mountains for a week. There was so much to talk about, including their trip to Calgary and meetings with Frank and Anita as well as many former colleagues and teachers.

They spent a lot of time in the mountains, discussing and debating the two books Eric and Louis had bought at the Goetheanum. It was an exploratory journey into Steiner's world with a quote from his book, *The Philosophy of Freedom*: "Each one of us has it in ourselves to be free in spirit, just as every rose bud has in it a rose."

Eric commented that there was a correlation between *The Philosophy of Freedom* and *Cosmic and Human Thought,* in the underlying structure of the Freedom of Philosophy by the World Outlook Diagram presented by Steiner. "This diagram explains the correlation between the worldviews possible for the mind and what is found in the outer world in the twelve signs of the zodiac and the seven planets," Louis added. "I'm not following Steiner's philosophy in this respect."

Eric replied: "This is where I also have a problem understanding Steiner's scientific cosmology." All four came to the conclusion that they would attend upcoming lectures to improve their comprehension and inform their desire to share their understanding with Frank and others with an expanded consciousness and a sense of humour.

The couples spent their holidays together, travelling to many countries and taking frequent local backpack trips with bicycles into the mountains. Both couples experienced great working relationships, setting examples for productive communication with business partners, colleagues, and superiors. As their independence grew in later years, the question of wanting more time to travel to foreign countries came up more frequently.

THIS TIME A LURE OF REMOTE AND ANCIENT CIVILIZATIONS

During a visit by Ursula and Eric with Louis and Sylvia in Zurich, Louis talked about a future opportunity, maybe in a couple of years, to work with another like-minded colleague doing research on new and extinct plants, birds, and butterflies along the confluence of the Amazon and the Rio Negro rivers, in the area around the city of Manaus, Brazil. A commitment in about six months would be necessary. Sylvia was very much in favour. This discussion coincided with Ursula and Eric's recent bicycle trip in the mountains. Ursula described this as follows, "Eric and I, for some time, have been talking about traveling to remote locations." While stopping at a viewpoint, Eric turned to Ursula to say he'd experienced a spark, something like a jolt, with an idea to travel into a remote and ancient part of the world to study village life. Ursula reacted with excitement. "I remembered my parents' trip to Namibia many years ago. My dad later mentioned that they regretted not having visited the southern and eastern part of Namibia, where pockets of Bushmen still live their hunter-and-gatherer lifestyles. Now we're considering this more seriously."

NAMIBIA, AFRICA—
HERE WE COME

The following months were filled with travels for Ursula and Eric to various places in Europe. Both were fortunate to be able to share these trips with their individual commitments. Within a year of their plans to travel to Namibia, they'd worked out a detailed itinerary into the interior.

A direct flight from Frankfurt to Windhoek, the capital of Namibia, was a popular route. The city of 250,000 is influenced by European culture. The languages spoken in Namibia are Nama, Herero, English, German, and Afrikaan. Namibia was a German colony from the 1880s to 1918.

Avis had their four-wheel Jeep ready, with warnings they did not get from the agency in Basel: Don't travel at night. The roads are narrow and sand dunes along them could be dangerous to slip into. There's no insurance coverage for sandstorm damage, like paint peeling off the vehicle from sandstorm warnings announced on radio. The steering wheel's on the left side. If you're not used to it, practise in

Siegfried Beckedorf

parking lot. Eric got N$s (Namibian and Botswana dollars) for the trip, as well as tourist information. He also bought a booklet about precolonial Namibia's history and tribes.

GOBABIS

Leaving Windhoek, they encountered a lot of wandering natives gathered in open areas, with fire pits smouldering. They were told that they were mostly Hereros coming in from the country looking for work. Gobabis, halfway between Windhoek and the Botswana border and about 200 kilometres east of Windhoek, was the first stop. The scenery there was dominated by endless savannas, with some brush and a dune-like contour, and some cattle on dry-looking land. Eric inquired about accommodation in this town of about 12,000 and if guides were available. A black lady in a coffee shop, a Herero, advised them to drive on a few more miles east on the Trans-Kalahari highway toward the border with Botswana, to an assembly of modern and not-so-modern accommodations where guides will pick up tourists for tours into Bushmen villages.

A lodge and camping place called Kalahari Bush Breaks with cabin-type looks and thatched roofs looked very interesting. They were impressed. There was a clean-looking bathroom, kitchen, and sitting area with two beds in a separate room. The lady introduced herself as of the Ovambo tribe. She spoke fairly good English. Ursula and Eric were happy and reserved the place for three days. "I will arrange for a guide to talk to you in the morning. You may park your car right in front and when the guide picks you up, you may leave the car here and the keys with us. We have a small restaurant and store right here."

Jacob, the guide, was a Herero. HE was tall, smiling, and had a mouthful of beautiful white teeth. He was also very talkative. He asked, "English or German?" Ursula replied, "We speak mostly English." Jacob added he spoke mostly English, too, but also speaks German. "There are many German-speaking cattle ranchers outside Hereroland where I live, just north of here. I work on an hourly basis, and like to be paid in N$'s at the end of the day. We will have lunch packed for us and water to drink. I'll take you right into Bushmen, or San country, as they are also called."

BACK INTO ANCIENT HISTORY, MAN'S EARLIEST ON RECORD

They travelled through dune country. The guide explained, "These are *grootduine*, Afrikaan for dunes. You don't see many animals, because they're widespread and gather around waterholes. We have antelopes, elands—which are like tall deer, wildebeest—which are like cattle, gemsbok and kudus, ground squirrels, and badgers. Their appearance depends on the time of year, whether it's rainy season or drought. Now after the rainy season, we should see some animals."

All of a sudden, out of the dunes after hours in glaring heat, a few huts appeared, scattered around some Acacia trees. Women and children moved between two fire pits, with smoke in the air. The women were busy piling up dead tree and shrub branches they'd brought in from the area around. Some were grinding corn in a bucket with wooden sticks with burls at the end. Jacob got out of the car and talked to the women, then turned around and waved at them to come. With a sweeping arm and a smile, he introduced the two whites. Big smiles were returned by one woman who talked to the other women, all of them very small in size, who also smiled at the visitors. Seemingly knowing the guide, Ursula and Eric were invited to sit down on stumps, while Jacob got lunch for them. Children slowly gathered the strangers to look at them. Ursula smiled at them and turned to Eric and the guide. "What a fascinating culture. So natural and easy-going!" Eric replied, "This experience alone is worth our trip." With a broad smile, Jacob explained, "You probably know that these people here are really our ancestors. Theirs is one of the first civilizations that walked our earth, some say about 50,000 years ago. Their language still has the clicking sounds that was their language before some of their people moved north to join other tribes and forgot about their roots, which includes us, the Hereros, and others. When the men come home very soon, you will see their tools and hunting gear and maybe some cut-up meat and bones, fur, or whatever."

Now he turned to the lady he'd first talked to. The woman spoke in a way not understandable with some clicking sounds. Jacob asked Ursula to ask any question she may have in English and said that he would translate. Ursula said with a smile, "I like your family, your children. I'd like to meet your men. We came from Europe to meet you." Jacob talked to the lady who replied with a lot of clicking and glances

Lifting the Fog

at Ursula and Eric. He then drew a few circles in the sand for the lady, explaining to Ursula and Eric, "I am telling them what part of the globe you came from." The lady talked to the other women and pointed at Ursula and Eric, swinging her arms and clicking. The children looked on in bewilderment. Eric could hardly believe what he was experiencing. "Ursula, this scene one has to hear and see in person. This civilization is dying out steadily!" Ursula was numb in her observation and nodded emphatically. "Eric, it seems time stands still here. What we are witnessing is ancient time."

Voices were heard, and the children got excited. Jacob was also excited, as a group of about ten to twelve men, including what looked like teenagers, appeared on the top of the dunes. The children ran toward them. Some men lifted their bows and shouted something. The arrival was met with a lot of clicking, laughing, and apparently sacred dancing, with singing in high voices. One of the men approached a teenager and gave her what looked like a green onion with a dead flower and some dirt. The girl was very excited. She ran to the women and showed them the plant, clicking and laughing. Then, a surprise to Jacob, she held the plant high for Ursula and Eric to see! Ursula waved at her and both of them were very touched. They clapped their hands toward the girl, who clicked to them, and smiled. Jacob translated: "It is her plant to take care of." Eric whispered to Ursula, "I am in awe. Love from the heart." Ursula nodded in excitement. Jacob mentioned that this plant was very important to them. It can be planted in the shade of some shrubs to spread out for use as a spice later.

Jacob had emphasized earlier that the women are highly respected, and "boss their men around." He met with what appeared to be the leader and pointed to Ursula and Eric, who were even more excited. The men unloaded their bows, arrows, tools, and their catch under the supervision of the women. Ursula and Eric joined them, and Jacob again asked questions. Eric was fascinated. "We came to visit, to know you and your families' way of life. I am honoured to meet you." Jacob bent down again and showed in the sand where the couple came from. The Bushmen smiled and clicked to Jacob, pointing to the fire. Jacob said, "he would like you to join them by the fire."

The leader waved his hand at Ursula and sat down, bringing his arrow along to show them. Jacob translated and said, "Look at the arrows made from bones and sharpened meticulously, the way it was done for thousands of years. The tips are filled with a special poison. The meat where the arrow hits is discarded. The bow showed again a very special way of being used. The type of wood is preferably acacia; tamarix; ebbehout, which is African; or tsawib, which is Herero. The leader got up and demonstrated how to use bow and arrow on a nearby woodpile.

After a while, everybody gathered around the two fires, the children crouched in between, the men telling stories. Jacob mentioned that the men were

Lifting the Fog

very lucky to get a good supply of meat, bones, and fur. The bones and fur were separated to be prepared later for use in arrows and hung up for drying for footwear and clothing.

Jacob reminded Ursula and Eric, "It is time to say goodbye. Best by walking over to the women first and the men after and thanking them and waving to the children."

The return trip brought a surprise as a large herd of wildebeest moved along at high speed on the top of a stretch of dunes. Jacob mentioned that they may have been scared by leopards or a cheetah.

Ursula and Eric were very happy with Jacob. Eric asked what he planned for the next day. "Let us visit one or two cattle farms owned by Bushmen who decided to become more sedentary. Hunting is getting more and more difficult, and more land is being used for farming. The government is favouring that development. I have an area in mind and will show you it on the map in the morning." They invited Jacob for dinner at the restaurant. The waitress recommended a menu of potatoes, maize or fruit salad, and wild or cattle meat. Jacob mentioned over dinner that he would like to show them a place nearby in Hereroland that was a typical village or farm, if they would like to see it. If they were travelling further south and wanted to see another Bushmen hunting-and-gathering place, he would recommend Mariental, which has a number of original Bushmen villages, similar to the one they'd seen, but a little different in language and lifestyle. "We

Siegfried Beckedorf

can talk about that tomorrow." Jacob shook their hands and said, "You are very nice people. You show real respect. The people showed that today." Both thanked him very much and paid him for the day. "You are an excellent guide. We will tell others, too. Thank you." Eric shook his hands.

Later, Ursula and Eric exchanged their impressions about the day. Eric was thinking about the Bushmen families, gathering the way they did tens of thousands of years ago. He compared the natives in Alberta with this scene. He believed that the Bushmen maintained their routines by not wandering and constantly following the need for food and wood, whereas the native Indians followed the herds of wild game for their needs. Neither civilization evolved as, for instance, the Europeans had. Maybe constant wars among the various tribes in Europe had played a role by improving their weapons and inventing new ways of settling down to constantly improving agriculture in ambitious ways and therefore offering more incentives for a different lifestyle? The treaties the white invading nations forced on the natives in North America also stymied the natives' lifestyles, taking away their nomadic way of life. Eric asked Ursula for her opinion on whether an intuitive prodding and growing awareness of an evolutionary process at work might affect the behaviour of primitive civilizations, like during the ancient empires of the Greek and the Romans, with advancing technology.

— 154 —

Lifting the Fog

Ursula tried to choose her words. She had no answer but she referred to today's more sophisticated world as compared to the world they'd experienced that day, which was less sophisticated, and had a lot of love, comfort, and care. Facts of cruelty, violence, and murder committed by organizations grown out of a tribal and religious background, for instance the Islamic State (IS), Steiner would probably look at a dark force that can't be confronted by military action because of innocent families used as shield by the IS, but only by raising awareness in the young people of the IS by patient infiltration of an educational process of a better world existing beyond the conditions caused by their leaders. A process to follow including giving the young people a chance to find ways of the human potential for change. Eric was quite impressed and suggested to share their conversation with friends and colleagues later.

Jacob was ready for them next morning. He laid out the travel plan. "We are driving a little closer to the border with Botswana. By the way, Bushmen are more concentrated in the southern part of Botswana. To reach them from Gobabis is a long way around. You mentioned you had Botswana dollars. If you want to exchange them, I'll give you Namibian dollars; it's about the same currency." Ursula and Eric had already decided to drive south to Mariental for more contact with the Bushmen there.

The dunes were present all the way through the country they passed through to get to the area where the Bushmen's way of life had turned to cattle farming. Since the 1950s, Bushmen were more or less forced away from hunting and gathering because of government-mandated modernization programs. There were some concerns about this program, but they couldn't be halted and they were considered necessary as game animals were being reduced by drought and over-hunting.

They arrived at a collection of huts and make-shift shelters, also sheltered from the sun by acacia and another species of trees. A fire pit with some pots on stone mounts was surrounded by women cooking, mostly grains like barley, maize, and roots. Some men and women seemed to be herding cattle toward a place where water was available in a lower area that was apparently dug out. A couple of men worked on the corral made of sticks interwoven and supported by fence posts. The corral out of wooden poles is meant to keep out predators and keep in cattle. Jacob talked to a man pointing to Ursula and Eric. He waved at them to come where women and children were gathered around some acacia trees and open fire pits. The women brought brush and dry tree branches toward the fire pits. Ursula and Eric found a shady spot to sit and children came very slowly toward them, led by the women. Jacob introduced the two with a lot of smiling. The women talking among themselves were now gathered around Ursula and Eric. Jacob asked Ursula again to ask questions and talk about themselves. The click-ing by the women talking to Jacob was quite lively.

Lifting the Fog

Jacob interpreted that they liked them and wanted them to talk to the children, too. Eric also asked some questions about how they feed the cattle with so little grass around. Jacob got the answer. "Right now, there are stretches of grassland here and there in between dunes where, just before the rainy season, grass and grain were seeded that was now used to feed. Later on, when it is very dry, they keep only a few cattle and sell some. They also move cattle around where patches of grass persist. These farmers are very poor and their wealth is only in the cattle they can keep."

Back on the trail, Jacob pointed to trees and said, "Those are places where grass can be found. These farmers are often on the move, with cattle being herded to such locations for a while. Food for the men is then brought to them."

Jacob laid out a plan for the next day with a map showing Hereroland adjacent to Bushmen territory. "I will take you there tomorrow on some trails not too far off the main road."

They arrived at an assembly of huts that looked similar to those of the Bushmen. The difference here, as Jacob elaborated, was that the Hereros have been farming for a long time. He was born on a farm further north. The grass was better there, and the soil had been worked and tilled for many years with equipment shared by large groups of farmers. "Most farmers here are still very poor and the men and women also get jobs in surrounding towns, like I did. About four families live on this farm here. They

Siegfried Beckedorf

share the cattle and work in groups. Each family has one or two huts. The large place with trees around and several fire pits is the gathering place for all."

Children moved and played in between the adults, always getting food from the pits where the pots were in use cooking meat and corn. Water containers like ostrich egg shells and carved-out wooden dishes were spread around. "The men come for food in between herding cattle, fixing fences and shelters," Jacob said, then turned to a group of women and men eating. He introduced Ursula and Eric. The Hereros looked up smiled and greeted with what sounded like "Welcome." Jacob picked up the lunch he had brought along, and they sat down with all the others on wooden logs and stumps. Jacob invited Ursula to say something and then Eric to follow. "I will translate." Ursula and Eric thanked them all for letting them meet their families, and said they were fortunate to be able to see how they live and that their children are so happy. The answers came mainly from the women, who wanted to know where they came from. Jacob drew a map in the sand, showing Switzerland and Namibia as closely as possible. The men also looked more attentively and smiled. One of them showed off some wooden and metal tools they used daily. One of the women showed them bright and colourful colonial dresses given to them by the Germans during colonial times. Each one of the women hand these dresses down from generation to generation. Jacob mentioned that the Germans had carried on a war with uprising

Lifting the Fog

Hereros and that there'd been many fatalities during that war, but that the Germans had later helped them settle down and raise cattle. After saying goodbye and thanking them all, Jacob, Ursula, and Eric nodded to the group and waved to the children, who looked with big smiling eyes and waved back.

On the way back, Jacob pointed to a crossing in the road, with a sign saying, "Steinhausen: 90 km." This road led to the north and west of Namibia, he explained. "This was once a German missionary, which attracted many farmers from Germany in the early 1890s. They established a nice little town. There are still a lot of German farms—even dairy farms—in the area. They have been and still are successful farmers, although some are selling their farms to Hereros, since their children moved way."

After an extended dinner, Ursula and Eric thanked Jacob for his excellent guide services and paid in Botswanan dollars. Jacob gave them back the balance in N$s. A handshake and "*auf wiedersehen*" put a big smile on Jacob's face.

MARIENTAL

Ursula and Eric decided to leave the next morning for Mariental with Jacob's advice on how to get there. The distance was approximately 250 kilometres. They would pass through two small towns: Leonardville and Aranos. The country they travelled through was a mixture of grassland, brush, and trees with dunes. It was very dry looking. Some cattle farms were scattered wherever grass and other vegetation were present. The first town, Leonardville, had one church, a small motel with a coffee shop, and some homes, as well as cattle farms in the area. Like so many towns throughout Namibia, Leonardville was also founded as a German Lutheran missionary. Its population was mainly a branch of Nama, Bushmen-speaking descendants of early Khoi inhabitants of Namibia.

They stopped at a coffee shop. There was nobody around, but a Bushmen lady looking out of the motel came over. They talked in sign language first, but the lady asked in German, "coffee and eating?" Ursula nodded. She left and came back with a can of coffee, cream, and rolls like pastry. There were only two

Lifting the Fog

tables. Ursula asked if she could also speak English. The reply was a show of two fingers, indicating little. Ursula and Eric communicated in German with some difficulty. It became apparent that this lady's family lived on a farm close by. She pointed at some huts and cattle. She also made clear that no one was in the motel. She was invited to sit down but pointed to the motel. Eric paid her, including a tip. She smiled, her teeth so white. Eric told Ursula jokingly, "No business stress here. Every moment nobody shows up." Ursula laughed. When leaving, they noticed some life—children chasing dogs and playing, and women around fire pits.

The country became a little more inviting after that, with grass and brush, and more cattle farms. They approached a crossing showing Mariental seventy-five kilometres to the right and Aranos a little further ahead. A sign announced: "Gemsbok National Park: 110 km." Eric suggested they head for Mariental. It was only a one-hour trip, and what a difference in the countryside. Green fields appeared after half an hour, as did berry farms, solid-looking houses, and what seemed like a warehouse, with little trucks moving boxes. They stopped and Ursula pointed at the literature about Mariental, where the population was 12,500 and the largest dam and reservoir in Namibia was twenty-two kilometres away. Most of the Bushmen people living here worked on their own farms or on cattle and commercial berry farms and dairy farms. The dam apparently brought prosperity to Mariental and its area. The literature also mentioned sheep and ostrich farming as being very popular. What a surprise! The town was founded in 1912 as a German Lutheran missionary.

Eric inquired about a motel assisting with guides. There were several that advertised Hardap Dam as specializing in tourists and watersport enthusiasts. One was recommended on the outskirts that also provided guides. It offered modern accommodation, a bed and breakfast, and kitchen facilities. Ursula suggested they drive there and check it out.

They committed to a three-day stay with a guide coming in the morning. Ursula was very pleased. Eric suggested a glass of wine with dinner to talk about the next few days. "Hold your breath. This is quite an experience!" Eric looked at the literature and got an idea. "Would you like to go for swim in the reservoir? It seems to be very popular. Tourists and locals seem to go there in great numbers."

"Sure," Ursula replied. "Maybe a couple of visits to meet local Bushmen. They seem to be somewhat different in their lifestyle, as Jacob said."

The guide introduced himself of being a San, formerly a Bushmen, by the name of Karl. "Are you German- or English-speaking?" Ursula answered that they spoke mostly English. "I live close by and have worked as a guide for many tourists, mainly German-speaking. I also speak English." His rates were about the same as around Gobabis, including lunch and dinner.

"I suggest we take a tour about fifty kilometres south from here to a cattle farm run by the original

Lifting the Fog

Khoi people, San. My own farm is not so original anymore. I work on berry farms if not guiding."

The effect of the Hardap Dam and Reservoir was quite noticeable on their drive west of Mariental. Karl pointed to the northwest. "The dam is about twenty kilometres in that direction. In between the Dam and Mariental there are many vegetable farms growing melons, maize, lucerne, and wine. Today, the dam is a popular resort with hotels and lots of sports like hiking in cool weather. We are now passing commercial berry farms. They use big equipment to cultivate and irrigate. Look at the game farm. This is an ostrich farm. Game farms including ostrich spread out in the mostly red-coloured soil with very few dunes and dry stretches. Turning south there is grassland and cattle ranches, some of them larger than the one-family type."

Gradually, the land became drier, and there was less farming. Karl mentioned irrigation that irrigation wasn't available there due to the distance from the dam. For some reason, most tourists only head for Hardap, ignoring the Bushmen villages off the beaten track. After a while, he made a turn to a large assembly of huts, all thatched and spread in a large circle. Karl had to stop the car to let a group of herders cross the road with at least fifty cattle. "These cattle are owned by several families who live in those huts in a half moon. They have fire pits in the centre. They also have some chickens. The children have a lot of playing room within the village area."

He parked away from the children and cattle, and walked to some women involved in grinding grain. They waved at him, and clicked a lot. More women came closer from the smouldering fire pits with children following them. Now he showed Ursula and Eric to follow him to a place where flattened logs served as a seating and eating area. The women stood around with children in between them. While Eric and Ursula stood by the benches, Karl talked Bushmen talk with the women, who pointed to the strangers. He'd told Ursula and Eric before that the Bushmen people around Mariental are not as shy. He thought this was due to their being not as poor as those up north. All women, now joined by some men, smiled when Karl introduced them and drew a large circle in the sand for the women to see. He clicked with them and made sure most of them could hear him. Turning to his cliennts, he said, "You tell them why you are here. Look at them, and I will translate."

Ursula and Eric stood in awe. Eric held Ursula's hand and said, quite emotionally, "What a moment." Ursula added, "Meeting you nice people living here so peacefully like your ancestors many thousands of years ago is overwhelming to us!" Karl smiled at the women and talked the Bushmen way to them with a great smile. A lady replied with her arms waving at all the others and then turned to Karl who interpreted to Ursula and Eric. "They are very happy that you came to talk to them. We like you, too." Karl seemed emotional. "They want to give you some fruit and share it with you." Ursula and Eric felt very

Lifting the Fog

close to them and showed it with their smile and by nodding thank you. There was a clicking sound from Karl.

Later over dinner, Karl asked if they had any other tours in mind. Ursula and Eric discussed a tour of the commercial farms, the berry and vegetable farms, and possibly an ostrich or other game farm. Karl liked the idea and said, "We can do that in one day. They are close together."

"I have taken many tours to farms northwest of Mariental. They get irrigation from the Hardap Dam, which was built in 1962. A number of German families from Windhoek bought land here before the dam construction started. The government sold the land for the purpose of agricultural development, with irrigation available in the future. Many South Africans, including Dutch people, settled here, as well.

The first farm is a berry farm—cranberries— that's owned by a German family. They worked hard to till the land before irrigation was available and are now very successful, employing a lot of Bushmen men and women and paying well. I've know them for many years. A European-looking house with red brick and wood siding appeared. They now have modern machinery and sell their berries all over Namibia."

Karl drove up to the house where a lady was talking to a group of San women. Karl spoke German to her. She replied in German, and waved at them. She told Karl he could take them around. A tractor,

— 165 —

tillers, and seeders were in the equipment shelter area . "They still do the picking by hand. The women are very fast and a picking machine is too expensive. Without irrigation, they would not have bought this land here."

Karl walked around long rows of berries full of fruit. "They are about ready to start picking." He pointed to the neighbouring melon and luzerne fields. "These look picked over. I'll take you to the other side where we come closer to maize fields and wine plantations."

A trip around the vegetable fields showed the extensive buildings of a manager residence, and many out-buildings, with equipment and storage shelters. A manager showed Karl the start-up of luzerne for ostrich feed and melon harvest. He pointed to the wine plantations and said that they were young wine stocks from this region that had been tested to be as good as South African wine. Karl drove around for closer visibility. Eric commented on the heat, amazed about the locals' ability to work in it so efficiently. Karl referred to the dam as the only source of water. "The Gobabis area is not even as dry as this land was before. We Bushmen can stand a lot of heat."

The next day, a visit to an ostrich farm was an eye-opener. Karl had access through a locked gate. The family-owned farm was enclosed and partitioned into sections by eight-foot fences. There was a large place with a residence, shelters for the birds, and storage for by-products from ostrich killed

Lifting the Fog

for meat, feathers, and various parts. Karl said the family was out for the day. Their foreman lived in a small house in one of the buildings. Karl spotted him in the field and waved at him. He came to the house and invited them to sit down in a shaded area.

The Herero man talked to Karl in English, smiling. "Thank you for bringing visitors to us. The family is in Mariental and I will tell you about our farm." He told them they had 900 black-neck ostriches, though the numbers constantly change. They buy and sell birds regularly. The day before, they had delivered about a hundred birds to the new abattoir in Mariental. Slaughterhouses are big business in the Hardap Dam area for meat. The abattoir sells the feathers to one company and skin to a tannery. The history of ostrich farming in Namibia goes back to around 1912. Wild ostrich were tamed in South Africa in the 1880s. Breeding stock was purchased in South Africa. Namibia's ostrich farms now total more than 43,000 birds over six months old.

"I will show a special section where we have breeding stock—it is still breeding season." An amazing display of male birds dancing and ruffling their wings. Bob drew their attention to a male digging a hole for the female to lay her eggs in." The female and male take turns sitting on the eggs, with the female doing the sitting in the daytime and the male in the night. Some birds can lay up to 100 eggs during the breeding season, with an egg being laid every one or two days. During this time, we have to be very careful because the males ostriches become very aggressive protecting both the female and the eggs." Pointing to other sections, he said, "when you came in, I put feed into different sections. We are fortunate to have luzerne fields close by. As a matter of fact, there is a big load of luzerne just coming in. Karl, you may want to show them around some more."

After a walk around, Karl said the two sons of the owner help him with the many chores to be done on a farm like this.

Karl asked them on the way back if they wanted to visit the resort area of the Hardap Dam, twenty kilometres from where they were. "You may enjoy that." Ursula and Eric liked the idea for the next day.

Over dinner, Ursula told Karl, "Eric and I have enjoyed your company very much. You have brought your culture, the way your people live, so near to us. You must feel good to be able to show your people to us in Europe and elsewhere in a way that allows us to learn how your family and children live in harmony."

"Thank you, Ursula and Eric. You are very nice people and show genuine interest."

Eric replied, "With our magazine, Ursula and I are working with people in Europe and America to promote better communication among families, students, teachers, and employers. Your work here shows you are maintaining your culture as best as possible." Karl became very thoughtful here. He looked at both of them and said, "Your messages to Europeans may help to prevent the speed at which

Lifting the Fog

our culture is becoming extinct. Our government does not do enough to help us."

Ursula and Eric made plans for the next few days. Eric told Ursula, "I did not expect a local guide to be a native. I am very impressed by the guides, the Herero, and even more with the two Bushmen guides. They are educated and speak different languages. I heard the lady in the hotel saying that the guides all live in their villages, are well paid, and have access to computers and phones. They have done tours for many years.

HARDAP DAM

They checked out in the morning and enjoyed the thirty-kilometre drive to the resort. There were green fields everywhere, along with farmhouses with large overhanging roofs for shade. What a different countryside. The surprise started growing as they entered the resort area. A huge lake—twenty-five square metres, according to the literature—and what activity! Anglers, waterskiers, tourists, and campers were everywhere. A parking lot shaded by acacia trees looked like an inviting spot to park the car. A number of people sat around tables along the lakeside shaded by large yellow Hapag-Lloyd umbrellas. Ursula suggested they stay overnight.

They looked around for a table and a couple invited them to join. "You are welcome to sit with us." Ursula noticed the couple drinking Elbschloss and asked if that was a good beer. "It is German beer from Hamburg. As you can see with the shades, Hapag-Lloyd is a Hamburg-based logistics company that's doing good business here." The middle-aged couple introduced themselves as German-Namibians from Swakopmund. "This is Angela and my name is Rolf."

Lifting the Fog

Smiling, Ursula said, "My name is Ursula, and this is my husband, Eric. We are from Switzerland." Rolf asked, "What made you visit this fairly remote place?" Eric explained their background and their reason for coming there. Rolf commented that most people from Europe visit Windhoek, the Etosha Wildlife Park, and Swakopmund. They visited the remote settlements of the San people, as well. "It's an emotional experience because their numbers are dwindling. The government could do more. The Chamber of Commerce and other private groups are trying to have the government do more to stop the eviction of the native people from their lands, resulting in the eventual extinction of an amazing culture."

Angela asked if they were staying overnight and Ursula confirmed that they were. Eric inquired about swimming. Rolf was not enthusiastic. "The water is nice and warm, but the waterskiers and the water sports interfere with swimming. It is not well organized and not separated. We are disappointed, in that respect. But there is also a public swimming pool, which we have used early in the morning. It is part of a lodge and is open for a fee."

Later, they confirmed the B&B and accepted an invitation for dinner by Rolf and Angela. Angela asked them to contact them when they arrived in Swakopmund. "There is a lot of detailed information about the original tribes and the history of Namibia in a museum. The Germans built the museum during their colonial time and made it an excellent

Siegfried Beckedorf

tourist attraction. It is kept up for that purpose." Rolf described the history of the Hardap Dam. "It is, for Namibia, an amazing project. It was financed by South Africa and Germany and employed a lot of natives in the construction. It brought a large agricultural development with it and employment for many natives. It improved the communication between the white and the native population.

The next morning, all four of them went for a swim. "This feels so good!" Over breakfast, Eric mentioned their involvement in what had started out as a student magazine and had become a large circulation of newsletters in the US, Canada, and parts of Europe, with emphasis of changes in the wind. "We are trying to improve communication among students, families, teachers, and employers."

"Interesting," replied Rolf. "Angela and I operate a local newspaper in Swakopmund. We are encouraging readers to voice their concerns in all affairs affecting their lifestyles, including telling the government to stop driving the San people out of their original habitats. We will send you a copy for further discussion." Ursula was excited. "Maybe we will have an opportunity to talk about this while we are Swakopmund." Angela and Rolf said they looked forward to their visit. "Happy trails, and enjoy the Etosha Pan and wildlife!"

DRIVING NORTH TO OTJIWARONGO

Their trip north toward Windhoek took them through an ever-changing countryside. Large herds of blue wildebeest, along with some gemsboks and antelopes, were visible among the red dunes and brush. The little town of Kalkrand—with only a service station, restaurant, and motel—did not show much life. The larger town, Rehoboth, which had 30,000 residents and was eighty kilometres south of Windhoek, showed a lot of activity. The population consisted mainly of Basters, an offspring, according to the literature, of Namas and Dutch settlers. Founded as a German missionary in 1845, it was baptized Rehoboth. The town attracts a lot of tourists visiting the rich fauna, marked trails, and lake of the surrounding areas.

The next stop was in Otjiwarongo, 200 kilometres north of Windhoek. They planned to spend a little time later in Windhoek before departing from there to Frankfurt. Small monkeys, warthogs running along in the ditches, and large herds of zebras came

Siegfried Beckedorf

in sight about 100 kilometres north of Windhoek. Termite hills were spread between cactus brush and rolling, steep, rocky hills. Otjiwarongo is the centre of cattle ranching in Namibia. Large cattle farms with small settlements account for Otjiwarongo's 30,000 inhabitants. The town looked very pretty and park-like, with a lot of blooming trees lining the street. A very inviting restaurant with outside seating and colourful shades looked inviting. The food included fresh fruit and European menus.

TSUMEB

On the way north, the countryside showed interesting vegetation, small pine trees, and rolling hills. A sign at the entrance to the city of Tsumeb said, "Welcome, Willkommen to the engineering hub of Namibia. Population: 15,000, the gateway to Northern Namibia and Etosh Pan and Wildlife Park." The literature explained that Tsumeb attracted a lot of German engineers, geologists, and skilled workers in the late 1880s and early 1900s for mining copper, railway construction and transporting copper to Swakopmund and freight back to Tsumeb. They build roads and provided utilities throughout Namibia.

Ursula remembered her parents talking about this city as still inhabited by many German families. Street and hotels had German names. A hotel called "von Ebb" looked inviting for spending the night and visiting the place. The museum featured a lot of German history, mining activities of the past, a mining history for diamonds, and various minerals and equipment. Hotel employees spoke German and English fluently, and the menu was German and intercontinental. A swimming pool added to

Siegfried Beckedorf

a comfortable stay. Ursula was excited talking to the attendant at dinner. "I am surprised how much of German culture and history are still present in Namibia after the South African government took over in 1918." The lady responded, "the South Africans made sure to have as many Germans stay as they could. They wanted to keep tourism going, which is big business for the government and the people." Expressing their fortune at being able to enjoy their trip, Eric felt good. "Every moment is filled with joy!" He kissed Ursula and said, "I love your enthusiasm!" The next day, they walked the well-treed streets—many with German names—and visited the museum.

HOBA METEORITE

They left for the Hoba Meteorite, 150 kilometres from Tsumeb. A sign behind the big chunk of shiny black rock explained that the meteorite hit the earth about 80,000 years ago. It was three metres long, up to one metre thick—one of the largest on record. Discovered in 1920, it was declared a national monument in 1955. The scientific description reads, "Nickel-rich Ataxit. No wonder many attempts were made to scratch or cut out some samples—none penetrated the solid mass."

TALERS, TALERS, TALERS

They decided to take a shortcut—a dirt road, according to the map. After half an hour, Eric was not sure where they were. They stopped the car on a narrow, sandy road with no trees for shade to look at the map. Suddenly, there was noise ahead of them and an old truck appeared. Three young black men jumped out of the truck and ran toward them. One of them pointed at the map Eric was holding while the other two grabbed Ursula to tie her up. She struggled to get loose and the other guy held Eric in his grip and with a rope. They called "talers, talers," the Afrikaan word for dollars. Eric pointed to the car, trying to tell them under the seat. On advice they'd received before they left, Ursula and Eric had put their passport and money in a bag tied around their waist.

With Ursula and Eric tied up, the three guys searched the car feverishly. Eric tried hard to untie the rope. With two guys under the truck and one bent over in it, they did not right away hear a truck approaching from the back of Eric's car. Two men jumped out and looked around and ran toward the car. By then, the black guys had taken notice and

Lifting the Fog

run to their own truck, spun around, and disappeared. Eric and Ursula got untied quickly. The two people, one black the other white, turned out to be ranchers looking for their cattle. They were told that this happened a lot in this area, that these guys and more of them wander around the countryside robbing tourists. They would have untied them as soon as they found money. "I will notify the police in Grootfountein, but there is little hope that they'll find them." Eric reached for some water for Ursula, who was in pain and upset, and thanked them. Eric was advised to follow them in a different direction for the main road leading back to Tsumeb. The maps are sometimes misleading, they told him, and it was best to stick to the main roads.

Eric and Ursula decided to stop in Tsumeb again to recover from the shock. They were still shaken by the event and had to share this very disappointing story with the waitress. She listened and replied, "I understand your shock and disappointment. Many tourists are concerned about unemployed youth trying to rob but not to hurt or kill. The police are unable to handle this situation—these young people are constantly on the move." They had become a little more relaxed and were given the good advice to travel only on marked roads. They also got some counsel regarding their travel to the Etosha Pan: "Do not get out of the car to look at the animals—they are wild." On the way to the Etosha Pan, Ursula was still in a state of shock, but Eric drew her attention to the vicinity of the game farm coming into view.

ETOSHA—WILDLIFE PARK

Etosha Pan was well advertised. Before even entering the park, you see giraffes moving around with their heads sticking out of the trees, looking down on the visitors. There are three stations within the park, which was used by the German military police—the Schutztruppe—during the colonial years as a defence against the marauding Ovambo tribes invading Namibia from Angola. Reconstructed to meet the growing number of tourists from many countries, they provided modern accommodation, restaurants, and educational facilities. There were three stations, 100 to 150 kilometres apart and spanning the entire width of the park. The rules were to come in no later than 6 p.m. and to leave any time after 6 a.m. Visitors were not allowed to leave their cars, and could only take photos from within the car. Wildlife there was indeed "wild," and as described in the literature, numbered about forty species, including lions, leopards, cheetahs, elephants, giraffes, rhinoceros, and zebras, along with many animals that roamed freely. Guards were everywhere, watching visitors.

Lifting the Fog

The educational section of the station elaborated on the unique evolution of the giraffe and its genes that allow it to feed from the top of large trees. It also observed that the amazingly long necks attracted females and was a monstrous evolutionary trend of the male.

Eric showed their pre-reserved tickets for three nights—for N$275 per night—at the first station, Namutoni. Three beautiful bungalows with six suites each allowed lots of space, including parking. A swimming pool provided nice refreshment after their adventure earlier. It was a busy place, and all the suites seemed to be occupied.

A couple from Edmonton shared a table with them and they exchanged stories late into the evening. The husband, a geologist, told them about an adventure they'd experienced near the diamond mines north of Luederitz, in a town on the Atlantic coast in the southwest of Namibia. Founded by a German merchant in 1864, it is today a very popular tourist destination. "We spent some time there. I was interested in the mineral and diamond mines north of Luederitz. The diamond mining area is fenced off and guarded everywhere. My wife and I were keenly collecting samples of minerals outside the fence when two guards approached us and said, 'You are under arrest, we are taking your samples. Please follow us to Luederitz.'

"We were dumfounded, but had no choice. We were interrogated by the police, who told us, 'You have taken diamond samples, which is violating our laws. If so confirmed, you will be kept in jail or pay a very heavy fine. You will be kept in custody until he samples have been checked.' Well, this took a day and a half. It was confirmed that there were no diamonds among the samples of our various minerals. There was a fine of N$250 for trespassing. I asked to talk to the geologist who checked the samples. I showed my credentials as geologist and explained that I looked for particular minerals in different countries as a hobby. I also explained that my father had been employed by a German mining company in the Windhoek area before WW II. He was interred, as this had been customary since Germany went to war with Britain and South Africa. He asked for my name and I told him. Then he said, 'Your father and someone else escaped into the mountains between Windhoek and Swakopmund, and they were found a year before the end of WW II and given their freedom because of their highly professional studies of the land and their experiences in the mountains. Your father and his friend had used the years in the inhospitable mountains living off the land and compiling notes about the natural area, including its flora, fauna, and geological features. I know, I bought the book they published later. It has been used by schools and universities. I will see to it that you can go without any fines. I wish you happy traveling.'"

In the morning, it did not take very long to watch a herd of blue wildebeest running at high speed, chased by a couple of lions. The chase took the herd far away, leaving behind a calf that was killed by the lions in a scene that was visible from the car. Ursula was nervous, but calmed down when Eric pointed at some giraffes crossing the road ahead of them. What a sight! The giraffes moved in a certain rhythm that seemed almost elegant. They did not pay much attention to the car. For a while, no other animals were visible until they arrived at a waterhole where large herds of zebras and gazelles were slowly moving away. The literature mentioned that large animal herds gather at nights around waterholes and slowly disperse after a few hours when new arrivals keep the traffic going. It also mentioned that there aren't many fights among the animals because they gather after having fed all day, and are thirsty, but aren't hungry. The prevailing animals coming into sight were large herds of elephants, zebras, élan, springboks, and giraffes. The countryside was mostly of savannah type, but that slowly changed to more hilly country toward the second station, called "Halali" (a German hunting call).

This camp was again a beautiful set-up, with bungalows, a swimming pool, and restaurants. The staff was very helpful to point out special events, such as a night show with big lights covering a large waterhole, grass, and brushland outside their camp, separated by a high fence. They gathered with many others to watch for about two hours as animals gathered around the waterhole. They must have gotten used to the lights. One particular incident was full of suspense as three lions strutted in a straight row along a path when a big rhino approached along the same path heading straight at them. Eric and Ursula held their breath! They could hardly believe their eyes when the lions moved upward of the path to let the rhino pass! A guard nearby explained, "They are not hungry and don't want a fight."

The next day offered a clear day, with a full view of the dry and salty Etosha Pan spreading for miles with hardly any vegetation and a blazing, misty sky above. A strange sight! The scenery now changed to more trees, mostly eucalyptus (gum trees), tamarix, and ebbehout, and tall grasses. Some trees looked petrified. Natives say, "These trees fell from the sky." A forester called them "living, petrified trees, but you should see them in early spring when they are blooming in different colours."

Along a stretch of savannah, their attention was drawn to large black vultures circling a clump of trees and sitting on branches, watching their turn. They spotted a couple of lions feeding on a dead zebra and hyenas waiting in the distance. A park warden was parked nearby, watching the traffic. There was no chance to take pictures with more cars following. Recovering from the sight, Ursula said, "Not a good sight, but carcasses are taken care of." After a while, they encountered another large waterhole. What a contrast to see huge herds of wildebeest, zebras, elephants, as well as probably most of the species in the park, shuffling, and waiting to get closer to the water fairly peacefully! Warthogs seemed to be most successful in getting to the water by moving quickly between the larger animals.

Lifting the Fog

A surprise awaited them in Okaukuejo, the third camp. A waterhole just adjacent to the camp enclosure surrounded by a large concrete wall was lit up for the guests as soon as darkness set in. Again, a great selection of large and small animals gathered. Ursula was inspired to sing along as they travelled, and Eric never stopped being amazed at the number of animals! Okaukuejo offered the same amenities as the other two stations. They stayed the next day until after lunch to enjoy the many educational programs and available literature.

ON THE WAY TO CROSSING THE OLDEST DESERT IN THE WORLD

The camp staff advised them not to leave the car at any of the small villages on the way to Swakopmund, and—better yet—to drive right through to Karibib. "There are wandering youngsters who rob tourists. Karibib is halfway and offers small restaurants for a break. The total time to Swakopmund is about five hours. Happy trails!" Very rough-looking rocky hills with small trees and shrubs surrounded the well-travelled road. Karibib has a population of about 3,800 and is an active mining and construction centre. A friendly black waitress with a white apron and head cover served them a refreshing lunch of fruit and chicken burgers with German beer.

Several little towns along the way did not show much life, with hardly any people in sight, with the exception of water pumps and windmills. After the two-hour crossing of the Namib, the oldest desert on earth, the blazing sun over its northern part turned

Lifting the Fog

to a hazy and misty sky, a sign of the Atlantic Ocean not far away.

SWAKOPMUND ON THE ATLANTIC

Before any settlements appeared, a sign pointed to a deserted locomotive, half covered in sand a few metres from the road. "Bis hier und nicht weiter," it said in German, which translated to "Up to here and not any further." Reference was made to Martin Luther's posting of his 95 Theses on a church in Wittenberg, Germany, in 1517 confronting the Catholic Church and sparking the Reformation. This locomotive apparently got stuck in the sand during the German colonial period. "What a sense of humour and what challenges they had to deal with the construction of the infrastructure in the desert!" Eric commented. Ursula added a funny thought. "Imagine the sandstorm peeling off the paint on that locomotive. That reminds me of the warning of sandstorms potentially hitting our car and to leave the radio on when we travel through the desert. It could have happened on the way here." Eric turned the radio on just as an announcement warned of a sandstorm sweeping through the Namib that was

Lifting the Fog

about 100 kilometres along the border with Angola. "That may not reach down to this area," Ursula commented, looking at the map.

A big sign—"Welcome—Willkommen—Swakopmund"—greeted the visitors entering the four-lane Kaiser Wilhelm Boulevard lined with fig palm trees and flowers on both sides along with well-landscaped bungalows. Side streets had German names like Moltke and Bismarck. The Bboulevard turned at the Atlantic Ocean, where it entered a park-like setting with palm trees and flowers along the coastline, along with hotels like "Deutsches Haus" and "Zum Gruenen Kranz."

Ursula spotted a bed and breakfast surrounded by tall rhododendron bushes called "Pension d'avignon," after a painting by Picasso. It was a beautiful and cool place with a French atmosphere and excellent service. Tired, but with a great smile, Ursula said, "Eric, hold your breath . . . and smell the flowers! I remember my parents talking about Swakopmund." Eric gave her a big hug.

A morning walk along the Atlantic among tall trees and flowers put them in love with this city of about 50,000, that was founded by German colonists in 1892. Well-preserved buildings like the Hohenzollern Hotel, the Railway Station, and the museum displayed Prussian architecture. The city is a very popular tourist attraction. The Atlantic Ocean provides pleasant summer temperatures. In the afternoon, they extended their walk along the ocean. A huge yellow tent structure with the name

Hapag-Lloyd, a Hamburg-based logistics firm, advertised a beerfest and the upcoming celebration of spring. Adjacent to the tent, a nicely landscaped city park attracted a lot of people, both black and white.

Early the next morning, Ursula and Eric started to drive into the Namib desert when a warning came over the radio "A sand storm is approaching the Atlantic coast north of Swakopmund. Travel not advised.." They returned to the city. They stopped at a coffee shop with a view of the ocean along the Kaiser Wilhelm Boulevard next to the Hohenzollern Haus to check their e-mail. An elderly gentleman approached them and said, "You are probably new here. Can I help you in any way?"

"Oh, yes and thank you," Ursula said. "We arrived here only three days ago." Ursula described their morning trip into the Namib and told the man about the "welwitschia" plant. "We planned to visit that area this morning, but returned because of the warning."

"It is amazing how many people don't heed the warning and pay a lot of money for repairs later. My name is Hans Becker. I have lived here almost all my life. I will be eighty next year. I can give you some information." Hans explained that he came from Capetown with his wife to set up his import-export business. "We sold it and bought a condo in the Hohenzollern Haus for our retirement." Ursula told him about her parents having visited Namibia. "We enjoyed our travels into Bushmen and Herero territory and the Etosha Pan. Quite an experience!"

Lifting the Fog

Hans was impressed. "Great, you have seen more of Namibia than most tourists I have met." He invited them for dinner at the Railway restaurant, and later to the museum where they could find out about the history of Swakopmund and its surrounding area. "I live in the Hohenzollern condo and can walk over there—would you like that?" Both Ursula and Eric were delighted and suggested the day after for dinner. He gave them his business card, which showed his membership in the chamber of commerce.

They made contact with the local newspaper office and met with Angela and Rolf, whom they'd met at the Hardap Dam near Mariental. Rolf showed them his latest newspaper and made reference to an issue that was very much in the news, the opening of a Waldorf school in Swakopmund. After a two-year effort, it was now financed by private interests for a small beginning. Angela suggested having lunch next door and discussing their mutual interests. The presence of the Goethe Institute was well received there.

The plan for the next day was to drive south along the coast to Walvis Bay, less than an hour away. Originally a British harbour dating back to the 1870s, Walvis Bay showed wrecked whale-fishing boats as evidence of its history. The hundreds of pink flamingos lining the beach areas made for a beautiful sight. Standing on one foot, they seemed to be watching tourists. On this day, a detour toward the desert seemed to be OK according to the morning news. They were heading for the area where the Welwitschia plants were located, and felt lucky to be able to visit these amazing plants with huge strut-like leaves and what looked like pine-cone growth around theirs core. The plants were all fenced in to prevent visitors from stepping too close and to keep the soil soft. One plant was labeled as being 1,500 years old, held moist by the Atlantic Ocean mist and an underground stream.

Another visitor pointed to the sky. "The wind changed suddenly to the north, I am heading back to the city!" Ursula and Eric followed the advice, and both vehicles were hit by the first waves of dust and sand. Before they reached city limits, they stopped, somewhat protected from the blowing dust over-head by large dunes. Eric noticed some paint peeling off the hood. The truck they had followed was hit as well, on the roof. About half an hour later, the wind died down, allowing for an inspection of the vehi-cles. They compared the damage. The other person pointed to the roof and hood of his truck. "That will cost a minimum of $2,000 to $3,000 to repair, match-ing the paint and repainting. No insurance company will cover this. The sides are OK." Eric figured about the same. The truck owner told them there was a body shop in Swakopmund, that they were experts and reasonable, and could handle this on short notice. "Please follow me. I am driving by there. I am Bert and live in Windhoek. I should know better, but this was totally unexpected for me." Both were

Lifting the Fog

able to make arrangements to have their vehicles repaired within three days.

Bert was very helpful in arranging for some items in the car to be taken to their B&B. They invited Bert for dinner at an Italian restaurant, which was Bert's choice. He explained that he was in the tree nursery business and had a main office in Windhoek. "It was my parents' business. My wife and I bought last year. My wife handles the business in Windhoek and I have a partner here in Swakopmund. I provide this office with some special products we grow in Windhoek." Bert was fascinated by Ursula and Eric's interest in early human life in Namibia and their work in Switzerland with the Goetheanum. "My wife, Angela, has a German background and is involved in the Goethe Institute, an organization very much involved with the Waldorf schools and Steiner's intuitive thinking and philosophy in general. I would like you to meet her, if you have the time when in Windhoek." That's great, we'll make sure to." Ursula and Eric parted and agreed to meet again when they picked up their vehicles from the body shop.

Walking along the shoreline the next day, they could hear music from the yellow tent. Eric peeked in and waved to Ursula. "Look, let's have a beer." An attendant invited them to come in. They joined a group of couples and singles from different countries. Two bands, a German and a British, were playing, each on opposite sides. With a nod, ladies in "dirndles" placed beer, buns, sauerkraut, and sausages in front of Ursula and Eric. There was no chance of starting a conversation as the music and singing along drowned out all talking! Some couples danced! Ursula and Eric joined in the singing and applauding for the music. During a break, they talked to the people around them and found out where they were from, like Australia, Sweden, France, and Germany. A few hours passed before Ursula and Eric got up to leave, waving at the crowd.

Walking along a commercial centre, they passed the coffee shop where they'd met Hans earlier and talked to him. He pointed to the Railway and Cohen Library building, where they wanted to meet for dinner, which he suggested they do in two hours. They walked over to have a look at this building. Restored from the 1890s into a modern restaurant and display of the colony's early railway days, the Cohen Library, is part of the attraction. Looking through the books, they spotted *When There is a War We Go into the Mountains*, by Henno Martin. "Look Ursula," Eric said. "This is the book here. The author is Henno Martin, the father of Herald Martin. Remember the couple from Edmonton we met in the first station at Etosha, Namatoni?" Ursula did. "It refers to the German title in here: *Wenn es Krieg gibt, gehen wir in die Berge.*" Ursula was excited "Let's buy it." It also shows the mountain ranges and canyons where the geologists lived off the land for over two-and-a-half years. It shows the sandy but solid road tourists can drive along between Windhoek and Swakopmund and look at the terrain." Let's

Lifting the Fog

look at that when we leave Swakopmund to see what's involved," said Ursula, smiling. "Maybe a little adventure."

The dinner was excellent. Hans and his wife, Elizabeth, were excited to have met them. "If there is anything you want to know for your trip, let me know." Eric replied, "We picked up a book," and showed it to Hans. "Oh, yes, I have it and have read it a couple of times. It is a legacy in Namibia."

"We are thinking about travelling through that area. It mentions a sandy but solid road."

"I have travelled on that road a few times. You have to prepare for it. There is no service station, no towns or villages. You see a lot of wildlife and some hunters, Bushmen, and others. Make sure your car is in good shape; your Jeep should do it. The book has a sketch with names of the entire terrain where they lived, gathered, and hunted. You can get a detailed map of the road. You can't get lost, though may be stopped by hunters. I have not heard of any attacks or robberies on that route. As a matter of fact, I heard of hunters helping people who got stuck. I heard you have to report when you leave Swakopmund and arrive in Windhoek. It's a shortcut, the paved road is about 400 kilometres and the shortcut will save some time. Sandstorms are only an issue for the first 150 kilometres, crossing the Namib. Get a report before you leave."

Eric remarked, "I feel we can do it, with enough supplies, etc."

After dinner, the couple gave them a tour of the railway exhibitions. There were truly remarkable photos of the very first years of building the railroad between Swakopmund, Tsumeb, and Windhoek. The couple surprised Ursula and Eric when they invited them to the Deutsches Haus, an elegant hotel and restaurant. "We are members of the chamber of commerce and the Visitor Club, promoting Swakopmund in trade and culture."

This dinner took place the evening before Ursula and Eric planned to leave for Windhoek. The restaurant was quite busy. The menu was in English and in German, and the waitress spoke English and fluent German. Light, classical music playing in the background gave this place a beautiful atmosphere. Surprisingly, its guests were mostly middle- and younger-aged. Hans elaborated about his younger years.

"During WW I, my father was interred, as this was the case everywhere. My mother, my sister and I had left a year before the war for Germany for a visit and could not return in time to Namibia. After the war, we returned and noticed Germans stayed to carry on their business and were supported in every way. The South African government realized the tourist potential for Namibia for people from different countries. Tourism is the biggest business for us. My own business in import and export was well respected by the chamber as well as by many segments of German business, culture, and education." Elizabeth added, "I can confirm this excellent relationship we have

Lifting the Fog

here in Swakopmund and Windhoek with locals of all levels." Ursula and Eric were very grateful and said they would like to stay in touch with Hans and Elizabeth about their own activities in Switzerland which may be of interest to their department of education and culture at the chamber. They parted with hugs and hopefully a *"wiedersehen."*

AN ADVENTUROUS SHORTCUT TO WINDHOEK

The next day, Eric filled out a report of their trip via the shortcut to Windhoek and made sure all supplies were updated, and to keep the radio on. Ursula, with map and sketch of the terrain in hand, gave Eric the approximate distance until the end of the desert. After one hour, they felt safe from sandstorms and looked at the sketch. It showed numbers from one to fourteen marking the places by their own names where the two geologists had wandered while living off the land, describing the places in German where they spent time for their field studies. The book they bought described the extreme temperatures, from ice-cold nights to very hot days. Finding water was one of the biggest challenges. It was amazing that these two survived for two-and-a-half years in this inhospitable environment! Their detailed study of wildlife, fauna, and geological features was highly appreciated by Namibian society and scientists. The book was made available to schools and universities in Germany, as well.

Lifting the Fog

They travelled along this terrain fairly close to the numbered locations and began to appreciate as authentically as possible the challenges the geologists had met and overcome.

They only encountered two hunters—one white person and his guide, a Herero. Eric showed them the sketch and the white person commented, "It's hard to believe how these guys survived! We travel in this Toyota four-wheel drive and go hunting fairly comfortably. I have a farm on the outskirts of Windhoek and know this country. You have only about seventy-five miles left until you get to the first settlement and then half an hour to Windhoek. Happy trails!"

A few switch-back turns caused Eric and Ursula to hold their breath. They also had to deal with a lot of dust and many potholes on the final stretch. They passed an old hut with a barn but no sign of life, and Eric mentioned, "This was probably a settlement at one time. I don' know what the hunter meant with 'settlement.'

The last stretch got them into the suburban area of Windhoek.

WINDHOEK,
THE CAPITAL OF NAMIBIA

Ursula spotted a bed and breakfast called
"Staufenberg Pension." They found it very comfortable and reasonable to stay for the three days before
they had to be at the airport. Frau von Staufenberg
welcomed them in English. "My name is Marlies.
We have a lot of German exchange students staying
here as well as tourists from many countries. Our
location is close to downtown and only a half hour
to the airport." Ursula gave a brief introduction of
their trip and Marlies replied, "My husband is at
our game farm near Otavi. He would be interested
in your experiences." After a swim in their pool,
Ursula and Eric highly appreciated this beautiful
and shady place.

The next morning, they walked to downtown
Windhoek, and were surprised to see newspapers
being advertised by people along the main street.
There was *Deutsches Tageblatt*, the "German Daily."
There were also many stores with German names.
They found the office where they had to report their

Lifting the Fog

arrival from Swakopmund on the mountain road. The man who gave them a receipt was very interested in their trip. They had a coffee in his office and were given more information. His Afrikaan dialect was very strong and he liked their interest in the native people near Mariental. "That is a good place to find originality!" Eric expressed his surprise about the strong German presence in Windhoek. The man replied, "it was a good thing many Germans decided to stay after the war. Tourism is number one here, thanks to them. They also attract a lot of international tourists and business."

The Windhoek Museum displayed history across Namibia before it became a German colony, including information on its various tribes and the many Missionary activities since the early 1800s. A beautiful park next to the museum also offered locally handcrafted wood carvings of any animal found in Namibia, as well as women's faces. It was beautiful work, and Eric bought one hiking stick with an amazingly fine women's face one it and another with a warthog— Ursula's favourite animal—rounded off at the very top. Eric didn't want to haggle about the price. Ursula loved the work and gave him a hug.

The meeting with Bert—whom they'd met in Swakopmund along with his wife, Angela, in connection with the sandstorm—was planned for the next day. They drove to their home almost hidden among big trees in a residential area surrounded by a protective wall and gate. They announced their arrival on an intercom box and were told to park their car inside. Bert explained, "Even though this is not such an expensive home, we've had many intruders breaking into new homes in the last five years. This is a new district and was planned with these walls."

Angela had prepared a lamb stew, with potatoes, roasted root vegetables, parsnips, carrots, spicy pepitas, and horseradish. Ursula gave Angela a hug. "What an effort, what a delicious meal!" Eric could not believe his eyes. "What a welcome!"

They spent all evening talking about the Goetheannum, the Waldorf schools, Steiner's work with Goethe in his early years, and the Goethe Institute. Eric explained his position in the field of architectural design, and Ursula described her role in the Goetheanum. Angela talked about her work with the Goethe Institute, a worldwide non-profit organization with 159 institutes. Ursula was well acquainted with the connection to the Goethe Institute. Bert, with his Italian background, was working part-time with his wife in the institute, whose excellent staff maintaied respect for German culture. They agreed to communicate with each other, especially with Ursula and the Goetheanum. What an exciting evening with these people! Ursula and Eric looked forward to an ongoing communication and their potential visit to Switzerland.

The next and last day, Rolf von Staufenberg and his wife, Marlies, invited them to a local Afrikaan-German restaurant. There, they exchanged their experiences. Rolf had made frequent trips to Switzerland, Austria, and Germany to promote

Lifting the Fog

African game farms and game parks. He suggested that Ursula and Eric write down their emotional experiences in the remote and original Bushmen settlements for publication in European magazines. He introduced them to the owner of the restaurant, a born Afrikaan who visited the natives in their settlements. He gave them a copy of a rough translation of the guttural sounds (clicking) of the Bushmen to Herero and English. He mentioned colonies made up of a mix of Bushmen and Dutch settlers who lived fairly close to the South African border. They maintain a different lifestyle that's more oriented to the white society. He offered a wild game menu with local root vegetables and sweet potatoes. It was another very interesting evening! The last of their travel to Namibia.

AT 30,000 FEET ABOVE AFRICA

At the airport, Ursula got a shock! She HAD left one of her two travel bags behind. Just as Eric reached for a phone, a lady from the Staufenberg Pension hurried to them with the bag. She was well rewarded. Eric experienced a challenge at the car return office. They tried not to accept the repairs to the Jeep for the sandstorm damage, even though the repair bill was approved by an insurance company in Swakopmund. Eric's determined attitude made them bow down.

At 30,000 feet over Africa, Eric turned to Ursula. "Hold onto this moment," he said. Ursula replied with a kiss. "And look into space. I cannot settle my thoughts about the state of our civilization in comparison to what I experienced with the Bushmen families. Is our society heading for too much materialism, too much comfort, and not enough respect for nature and the environment?" Eric replied, "Such thoughts have occupied my mind many times during our trip. When I think about the genuine smiles of

Lifting the Fog

the women and the happy children playing between them, looking at us with big eyes and shining teeth, I felt good in returning their smiles, assuring them we are part of their world, are friends and not threats from the outside."

Ursula nodded her head. "Alone, the action of one of the men returning from their hunt and handing a little plant, an herb, to a maybe ten-year-old girl who held it up high and waved it at us, showed me that these people are as highly educated as we are in many ways in our highly sophisticated civilization. Our Bushmen guide explained that the girl would plant this in a shady spot for future use as a spice. It was a sign of their awareness of and respect for nature in surroundings of sand and sparse growth. I will remember this as a highlight of our trip."

Eric was moved. "I felt good when I witnessed this moment, knowing these people have a healthy mind and live in the moment, and aren't sidetracked by the kind of numberless thoughts that go through our minds in our society. It also gives me hope that these people, especially their children, have a chance to grow into a different world, and to be respected for their originality, not to lose their inborn qualities." Ursula agreed. "I will integrate my experiences of this visit to the ancient civilization in my work at the Goetheanum, as much as it creates understanding and respect for these cultures."

BACK IN SWITZERLAND

While they were landing in Frankfurt and changing planes to Basel, they met a director of the Goetheanum in charge of international relations. Ursula turned to Eric, "Do you remember, we met for lunch at the Goetheanum when you had just arrived from Calgary?" It dawned on Eric. "Yes, I do. Nice seeing you again. Things have changed quite a bit since then." The director explained that he had just returned from Kairo and Ursula filled him in on their trip to Namibia. He reported on a few things that had happened since they left for Africa. "Ursula, now that you have gained a lot of respect for your input, we, the board of directors, will offer you a position where you might at your convenience, internationally. You will get the details when you get back to the office. I hope you can stay around for a while." Ursula was surprised. "Very interesting, indeed. Thanks for telling me." He offered them a car ride to Dornach.

In the evening, Ursula lifted her wine glass to Eric and said, "Hold your breath. Was this all a dream?" Eric pinched her. "No, this is a moment to celebrate!"

Lifting the Fog

They recalled some highlights of their trip, and Eric said, "It does all seem like a dream."

Later, Eric mentioned that he was in a similar position in his architectural firm. "Ursula, you may be travelling a little more if you accept that position. I am OK with that since I also have to make a decision for an advancing role." Ursula said, "an international role with the Goetheanum as a lecturer is an amazing opportunity to get a personal note into its content." Eric, pointing at his head, said, "I remember Toni asking me some time ago to make other firms abroad more aware of the uniqueness of Steiner's designs in their work. That could possibly mean making our trips overseas together." Ursula was excited. "What an interesting opportunity! Let's discuss this among ourselves first before I go back to the office."

A message was waiting for them when they got home. Sylvia and Louis wanted to visit them in Dornach the coming weekend. It was a wonderful visit. Sylvia was bubbling with excitement, as she'd been appointed assistant principal at her Waldorf school. Louis was also happy in his job. He'd accepted, with Sylvia's consent, a one-year research assignment in Brazil in possibly a year or two. Even though all of them had not been bicycling for some time, they managed a trip into the mountains. When they arrived at their favourite viewpoint of the panorama of the Swiss Alps, Ursula led their common enjoyment. "Hold your breath. How beautiful!"

Siegfried Beckedorf

Later, sharing their recent mutual experiences, Sylvia was quite touched when Ursula described their very close meetings with the Bushmen families in their original settlements. Louis was happy to report that their student magazine had found acceptance in many European universities. Sylvia asked Eric and Ursula to give her a summary of their experiences and contacts they'd made in Namibia for the magazine. Frank would get a copy, as well.

A GREAT MOMENT—
A NEW ROLE IN SHARING
STEINER'S PHILOSOPHY

At the meeting with the board of directors, Ursula was overwhelmed by the praise she received about her competence in representing Steiner's philosophy and her participation in lectures. One director pointed out, "You seem to live your work with enthusiasm, and that is mirrored in comments we receive from lecture attendants." A detailed offer of international lectures was given to Ursula for consideration, with time to make a decision.

Ursula accepted the offer within a few days and received support in her suggestion to travel with her husband in his international work as much as feasible, as he had a similar offer to meet commitments for meetings.

INTERNATIONAL EXPERIENCES

The first assignment took place in Toronto, followed by Calgary and Vancouver. It went well for Ursula. In a question-and-answer period after her lectures, Ursula responded to questions regarding the kindergarten and elementary Waldorf education models thus:

"In the Waldorf kindergarten, children are cultivated and work in support of the deep and inborn natural attitude, belief, and trust in, and basic reverence for, the world as an interesting and good place to be. In the lower grades in elementary school, this focuses more on using artistic elements in different forms, not primarily as a means of personal self-expression, but as a means to learn to understand and relate to the world, and to build an understanding of different subjects out of what is beautiful in the world in the broadest sense of the word.

Eric was able to attract good audiences of architects and builders in those Canadian cities to his introduction of Steiner's unique architecture and

Lifting the Fog

principles. He put a number of firm names on his list for future contacts as well as names with special interests in respective "round" architecture in Canadian cities.

Ursula followed a similar pattern in the States as in Canada, for her presentations in a total of thirty cities over a period of several years. She did encounter a few challenges from people, including from some who came from a background of viewpoints that differed substantially from Steiner's. She also got some opposition from fundamentally religious groups about Steiner's lectures, "Human and Cosmic Thought," especially regarding his statement that "the human being can be seen as a thought by the Hierarchies of the Cosmos." Ursula advised these people to contact the world centre at the Goetheanum in Switzerland for special lectures on the internet, or in person at Dornach, Switzerland.

Eric could not always follow Ursula's itinerary, but in most major locations in the US they were able to meet, and also for very relaxing periods.

The lectures expanded over several years to other locations like Australia, New Zealand, and Japan. These talks allowed them a lot of beach and hiking time.

A CHANGE OF PACE

After many years of travelling and giving talks, Ursula and Eric became aware of a needed change. They were both offered advisory positions as a pre-retirement opportunity in Switzerland, whenever they desired. This suited them well in terms of their bicycling and hiking trips in the mountains, at times in the company of Sylvia and Louis.

Ursula found a niche in marketing lectures in Switzerland and elsewhere, and Eric joined other architects in Europe and North American who had projects with "round" design and architecture.

CELEBRATING URSULA'S LIFE

After her eightieth birthday, Ursula showed signs of failing health. A few months later, very surprisingly, she made her transition peacefully in their home with Eric present. He felt shocked, sad, and strange about accepting this sudden loss.

A celebration of Ursula's life was attended by relatives, friends, and people from many countries. All paid tribute to her dedication to Rudolf Steiner's philosophy of individuality and freedom.

THE CALL OF THE FOOTHILLS

A few months later, Eric travelled to Calgary for a visit. Hiking in the foothills and mountains, he had a strong feeling of being home again. The "four strong winds of Alberta" made him decide to move back to Calgary for a change of pace.

AN EXPANDING NETWORK WITH EMPHASIS ON SCIENCE

The network of the students' newspapers had expanded steadily,y with regular feedback over many years. Eric liked the feedback, especially from students from universities all over, as well as communication with teachers, parents, and others concerned about a good understanding between all parties. Many offered their individual situations. Other networks and media groups contributed to a growing movement open to science, new ideas, and the maintenance of the human spirit in a world of rapidly advancing technology and science. This widened their influence among lecturing authors.

At a meeting in Denver, Frank shared with Eric and Louis and the newsletter group that he had taken a membership in Science and Non-Duality (SAND). The organization emphasizes "the true meeting of science and spirituality." Its mission is to forge a new paradigm in spirituality, one that isn't dictated by religious dogma, but that's based on timeless wisdom traditions of the world, informed by cutting-edge science, and grounded in direct experience.

Eric presented a summary of a book, with reference to Frank's membership in SAND: the New York bestseller by internationally known theoretical physicist and author of nine books Lawrence M Krauss, *A Universe from Nothing: Why there is something rather than nothing*."

Eric added his own interpretation of science's role in his recognition of the beauty of a rainbow or a snowflake. Science, he said, puts this more into focus based on the simple, elegant laws of physics. "Let us not overlook the fact that scientific research adds to our enjoyment of nature and the appreciation that the human spirit is alive. Philosophy is wisdom with practical knowledge harmonizing with day-to-day living. Knowledge is science based on hard evidence. Finding common ground between wisdom and science is a challenge for us all.

In honour of their contributions to the newsletter now published in North America and Canada, Frank, Eric, Louis, and their wives were invited to a gala dinner that was attended by many professionals in the field of education. It was a meaningful event that was enjoyed by all, and about which a story was published in the newsletters.

ACKNOWLEDGEMENTS

Thanks to Lloyd, my son; Linda, my daughter-in-law; and Cyr, my grandson. Special thanks to the Beckedorf and Bourdage families in Canada, USA, and Germany; the Waldorf teacher, Erin, and student, Annie Beckedorf, for their support and encouragement in the preparation of the manuscript; and the previously mentioned Barb Howard, president of the Writers Guild of Alberta.

Printed in Canada